RESILIENT
FAITH

A Devotional Commentary
on the Book of Daniel

S. K. Fine

Every effort has been made to acknowledge the sources used in putting together this devotional. If any source was missed, it was unintentional. Please notify AsherPub@pm.me of any omission, and it will be corrected if an updated manuscript is submitted to the printer.

Photocopies of the chart on page 10 and a single day's devotional are allowed for promotion of private or church-based Bible study. To request additional reproduction permission, contact AsherPub@pm.me.

Asher Publishing, Iowa City, Iowa
Asher Publishing, 2023

Original cover art design by Christoph Truemper.
Interior design and typesetting by KUHN Design Group | kuhndesigngroup.com

Publisher's Cataloging-in-Publication data:
    Names: Fine, S.K., author.
    Title: Resilient faith : a devotional commentary on the book of Daniel / S. K. Fine.
    Description: Includes bibliographical references. | Iowa City, IA: Asher Publishing, 2023.
    Identifiers: LCCN: 2023910863 | ISBN: 979-8-9885482-7-0 (paperback) | 979-8-9885482-0-1 (hardcover)
    Subjects: LCSH Bible. Daniel--Devotional use. | Bible. Daniel--Commentaries. | Devotional calendars. |
        BISAC RELIGION / Biblical Commentary / Old Testament / Prophets | RELIGION / Christian
        Living / Devotional
    Classification: LCC BS1555.54 .F 2023 | DDC 224/.506--dc23

Library of Congress Control Number: 2023910863

*This book is dedicated to Jesus Christ,
my personal Lord and Savior.*

*A special thanks to my parents,
who both believed I would write a book someday,
and to my sister, who beat me to it.*

CONTENTS

INTRODUCTION

G od is Sovereign and the Messiah is King. This is a central message of the book of Daniel. From there, Daniel is both about faithful resilience amid adversity and prophetic hope for God's good judgment and tangible reign. It is an ongoing message that speaks to each generation of believers in all parts of the world, encouraging us to persevere no matter the trial or obstacle; reminding us that each nation-state is temporary, but God is eternal; and comforting us with the promise that God is with us—we are not alone.

PURPOSES OF THIS BOOK

- Make the book of Daniel accessible in bite-size pieces for someone new to reading prophetic literature.

- Recognize the historical and cultural context in which the visions of Daniel take place.

- Disciple the reader in the basics of Christianity while traversing through a book of the Bible.

- Assist the reader in making a spiritual connection with God.

HOW TO USE THIS BOOK

The Christian practice of sitting down regularly to thoughtfully read Scripture and pray helps the believer internalize biblical faith and connect with God. It reprioritizes our values and gives us direction and strength for living each day. *Resilient Faith* is intended to create a simple roadmap for doing this in partnership with the writing of Daniel.

Often a person selects a certain time frame each day to put this Christian practice into action. For some, it is first thing in the morning when they wake from their slumber. For others, it is during their meal break at work. For still others, it is in the evening before going to bed. I imagine you, the reader, sitting down at a designated time each day with a copy of the Bible—paper or digital—a cup of your favorite beverage, and a copy of this devotional commentary. You then pray, inviting God to give you guidance and understanding before reading the selected passage from Daniel or a related book that you find listed under that day's devotional heading. After reading the selection, I imagine you continue by reading the devotional and then writing down your thoughts in response to the questions that follow. This slower, more deliberate reading of Daniel comes with its own unique blessings.

On the other hand, I recognize that still other readers will encounter the words on these pages more intermittently. Perhaps if you are this reader, you will keep a copy of this devotional in your bag or vehicle and will pick it up during one or more of the many times of waiting during your day. Perhaps it is while waiting for a business associate, or while sitting in yet another medical waiting room, or maybe while waiting for a child to complete the practice of a sport or instruction in an art. In this moment of pause, I hope you will find appreciation for the omnipresence of God and recognize that God is waiting for you to turn your attention toward the Great I AM.

However you choose to interact with the Word of God using *Resilient Faith* as a guide, I pray that you may be blessed with a greater appreciation of who God is and how your life might be molded by an ongoing relationship with the Sovereign Grace.

To describe the "how" more succinctly, each day:

1. Pray, asking God for understanding and, if appropriate, personal life application of the reading.

2. Read the passage from the Bible listed at the top of each day's devotional.

3. Read that day's devotional commentary from *Resilient Faith*.

4. Respond to the reflection questions. Write your answers in the provided space on the page, in the margins, or in a separate journal.

5. Pray again, thanking God for the time you spent in God's Word.

The devotional commentary is designed for you to listen deeply with each day's reading and to encounter the text with thoroughness and curiosity. You will note that some verses of Daniel are repeated in more than one day's devotional. You will also notice that it may take as long as two weeks to cover just one chapter of Daniel. This is intentional, as we do not want to rush through our reading and miss the beautiful nuances of the text. We want to take the time to slow down and really listen. The slow, repetitive reading of Scripture is known as "meditation." I also encourage you to re-read the entire chapter on the days of "Action" found at the end of each section. You will find the additional "Go Deeper" reading at the end of each day for the more adventurous and experienced Bible reader who has chosen to take the time to dig deeper into the theme presented for that day's passage from Daniel.

SMALL GROUP STUDY

This devotional commentary is designed for the individual but can also be used by two or more people as a study. Each chapter of the book of Daniel is covered with a blend of devotional thought and historical, cultural, and theological commentary that can be ripe for a group discussion. When planning your group study, plan to meet for a minimum of sixteen weeks. Most weeks, you will cover one entire chapter of the book of Daniel. There are four chapters that each take two weeks for study: chapters 2, 4, 7, and 11. Please note, the chapters are not to be studied in the order that they appear in the Bible. A planning chart is provided on the next page to help your group plan for your study. Some groups may decide to have members take turns each week hosting or facilitating the group's discussion.

When you meet, in addition to reflecting together on the "Action" items that conclude each chapter, invite each participant to select two or three questions from the daily devotions they read to bring to the group for discussion.

Date Group Meets	Location of Meeting	Chapter of Daniel to Read in Advance	Daily Devotions to Discuss at Meeting	Conversation Facilitator
		Daniel 1	Days 1 – 7	
		Daniel 2	Days 8 – 11	
		Daniel 2	Days 12 – 18	
		Daniel 3	Days 19 – 25	
		Daniel 4	Days 26 – 29	
		Daniel 4	Days 30 – 33	
		Daniel 7	Days 34 – 40	
		Daniel 7	Days 41 – 47	
		Daniel 8	Days 48 – 53	
		Daniel 5	Days 54 – 60	
		Daniel 9	Days 61 – 67	
		Daniel 6	Days 68 – 72	
		Daniel 10	Days 73 – 78	
		Daniel 11	Days 79 – 83	
		Daniel 11	Days 84 – 88	
		Daniel 12	Days 89 – 94	

SCRIPTURE, SOURCES AND ADDITIONAL COMMENTARY

You'll find Scripture references throughout your daily readings. The references that are not part of the daily reading will be noted with an in-text listing of the book, chapter, and verse(s) where it can be found. Additional author commentary can be found in the footnotes. Sources used are recognized in the bibliography and endnotes. You will find an index of all Scripture references at the end of the book.

MY PRAYER FOR YOU, THE READER

Gracious and Sovereign God, may your blessing of grace, wisdom and discernment, and abiding presence be with the readers of this devotional commentary, that they may find time to meet with You and encounter Your presence in the holy words of the Bible. Through Christ Jesus and in recognition of His crucifixion, resurrection, ascension, and future return, and in hopes of new life in Christ for the reader and myself, I pray. Amen.

ABIDE WITH ME!

Hymn, by Henry Francis Lyte

ABIDE with me! Fast falls the eventide;
The darkness deepens: Lord, with me abide!
When other helpers fail, and comforts flee,
Help of the helpless, O abide with me!

Swift to its close ebbs out life's little day;
Earth's joys grow dim; its glories pass away:
Change and decay in all around I see;
O Thou, who changest not, abide with me!

… Come not in terrors, as the King of kings;
But kind and good, with healing in Thy wings:
Tears for all woes, a heart for every plea.
Come, Friend of sinners, and thus bide with me!

… I need Thy presence every passing hour.
What but Thy grace can foil the Tempter's power?
Who like Thyself my guide and stay can be?
Through cloud and sunshine, O abide with me!

I fear no foe, with Thee at hand to bless:
Ills have no weight, and tears no bitterness.
Where is death's sting? where, grave, thy victory?
I triumph still, if Thou abide with me…

DANIEL 1

INTRODUCTION

TREASURES

READ ISAIAH 39:1–8

Daniel's story begins with the fulfillment of a prophecy. The history behind that prophecy is fascinating. His ancestor, good King Hezekiah of Judah, makes the mistake of boldly showing off all the treasures of his kingdom to his guests, representatives of the son of the King of Babylon. Who shows a potential enemy all of one's treasures? The prophet Isaiah calls Hezekiah out on his foolishness.

Isaiah explains that according to God, who understands the human heart, a time will come when Babylon takes away everything the king has just revealed to them. Even some of Hezekiah's descendants will be taken away to become eunuchs in the palace of the Babylonian king. Who are those eunuchs? In Daniel 1:3–7, we learn that they are our main characters: Daniel (Belteshazzar), Hananiah (Shadrach), Mishael (Meshach), and Azariah (Abednego). Daniel and his friends, against their desires, fulfill Isaiah's prophecy.

Perhaps the understanding that God had known a hundred years prior that this would be Daniel's fate gave Daniel the courage and the faith we see modeled throughout this story. In Daniel, we see a man who is confident in his identity, in God, and in his relationship with God. He is a royal who is called to serve and witness to foreign kings. His service results in them recognizing the sovereignty of the God of Israel. This is much like the ministry of his ancestor King Hezekiah, who ended the worship of foreign deities and proclaimed the worship of Yahweh (God) alone.

As we read through the book of Daniel, we are not surprised to see the angels identify him as "treasured by God." This is not only because of his purity of devotion but also his courage and boldness. He is indeed one of the many holy treasures stolen by Babylon.

TIME OF REFLECTION

Go Deeper: 2 Kings 20:12–19

King Hezekiah brags about the treasures of his household, which include items from the Temple and his military's armory. Why was this a foolish thing to do?

In a similar manner, how is it foolish of us to brag about our material treasures, our spiritual treasures, and those things that are meant to protect us?

Daniel was taken away to Babylon as a prisoner. Yet, his faith remained resilient. How would knowing that your difficult circumstances were part of God's plan help you to be resilient in your faith?

HISTORY

——— READ DANIEL 1:1–2; JEREMIAH 25:1–14 ———

I t is truly amazing how the parts of the Bible fit together, particularly the various components of the Old Testament. If you have trouble understanding the Old Testament outside of the books of Torah (Genesis, Exodus, Leviticus, Numbers, and Deuteronomy), then take some time to study the history of the Babylonian captivity of the Jewish people. Understanding this piece of history gives much of the writing a historical context and meaning. Here is a brief summary:

The book of Daniel begins by placing Daniel at the very beginning of this historic moment. In verse 1, we read, "In the third year of the reign of Jehoiakim king of Judah, Nebuchadnezzar king of Babylon came to Jerusalem and besieged it."[1] Earlier, Jeremiah the prophet proclaimed that Nebuchadnezzar would come and conquer Jerusalem if the people of Judah did not turn from their evil ways and return to worshipping God alone. He foretells that this time in which the people of Judah are taken out and away from Israel will last seventy years. This is known as the Babylonian captivity, the Exile, or the beginning of the Diaspora. Daniel and his companions are among the first of three deportations from Judah. (You can learn more about Babylon's conquering of Judah and the destruction of Jerusalem and the Temple in 2 Kings 24–25.)

In the beginning verses of Daniel, we learn of the movement of three symbols from Jerusalem to Babylon.

1. The evil King Jehoiakim is taken from Jerusalem in bronze shackles (2 Chronicles 36:5–8). Not much later, we see the same happen with his young heir Jehoiachin. Jehoiachin is placed in prison for thirty-seven years. It is not until he has served his time that he is released and returned to a place of honor in the king's court (2 Kings 25:27–30). We see in the exile of Jehoiakim and the imprisonment

of his son a symbol of God's judgment and correction of those who are unfaithful.

2. In verse 2, we are told that the Lord also handed over or delivered to Babylon the vessels from the house of God. These were preserved, although misplaced, in the treasury set aside for Babylon's false god, symbolizing the people's misplaced trust in foreign gods. In preserving these vessels, God ordains their future use in a rebuilt Temple in Jerusalem, thus giving a symbol of hope of a future return and restoration.

3. Finally, four young Israelites are chosen to serve in the king's court. These four represent the faithful of Judah who will be preserved as a remnant of those who will someday return to the Promised Land. They symbolize God's protection and faithfulness to the people of Israel.

TIME OF REFLECTION

Go Deeper: 2 Kings 24–25

How in your life have you seen God connect the dots between people and events to give you a hope-filled future?

What have you learned about the Bible that has helped you trust it as a source of Truth?

When and where in your life have you experienced a time of exile? Was this self-caused, caused by an external source, or a combination of the two? How did you get through it?

ADAPTATION

—————— READ DANIEL 1:3–8; LEVITICUS 11:44–47 ——————

Pursue the well-being of the city I have deported you to. Pray to the LORD on its behalf, for when it thrives, you will thrive" (Jeremiah 29:7). In his letter to the exiles of Babylon, sometime after Daniel was taken there, Jeremiah gives the instruction to the exiles to care for their new community. The question, "How is one to live in Babylon?" must have been on many people's minds. The Jewish people understood themselves to be set apart as holy to the Lord. Without the Temple in which to worship God, those habits that set the people apart from all other nations became more critical to maintain their unique identity as God's chosen, while adapting to and integrating with the culture around them.

We see this in Daniel and his companions. They are included in a special training course that will allow them to become advisors to the ruler of Babylon. They accept this instruction, learning how to conduct themselves in court and as government officials; learning the languages, script, and literature of the empire; and studying international relations.[2]

They also accept the new names given to them. This may be surprising to us modern readers of faith to see their willingness to no longer be called by their given names, names which honored the name of their God, only to instead be called names that honored the gods of Babylon. Yet this seems to have been a common experience, as even Joseph a thousand years earlier accepted the Egyptian name Zaphenath-paneah (Genesis 41:45).

But Daniel did draw the line when it came to what food he was willing to consume. The ancient writer Leander of Seville compared the king's food to bait on a fishhook.[3] God had given Israel specific instructions about what they could and could not eat and even how to kill and cook it. The diet of the Hebrew people made them distinct and set apart (a.k.a. "holy") for God. To not adhere to this diet was to deny the holiness of God and to defile oneself. So Daniel requested to adhere to a different diet, a diet that would honor the one true God.

TIME OF REFLECTION

Go Deeper: Leviticus 11; Deuteronomy 14:1–22

Daniel and his companions' resilience came from a combination of non-circumstantial adaptivity or "adaptitude" and submission to the sovereignty and wisdom of God. Two beneficial traits we can integrate into our own lives in our own changing circumstances.

What is a struggle, breakthrough, or pattern in your life that requires you to adapt?

How are you doing at adapting?

How would trusting that God is sovereign in your circumstance flex your ability to adapt?

How are you remaining faithful to God and honoring God in your present circumstance?

COURAGE

—— READ DANIEL 1:8–16 ——

Courage starts with small steps. It begins with confronting our peer who speaks ill of another and asking them to no longer do so. It grows as we choose to act differently than our culture when our culture asks us to indulge in sinful desires. It comes from a place of deep humility and trust in a Providence greater than us. Courage is a muscle we train so that when the time comes for us to stand up with valor, we might be able to answer that call.

The chief eunuch who oversaw Daniel did not have courage. His fear of the king was greater than the compassion he felt toward the men under his care. But his lack of courage did not inhibit Daniel from expressing naïve perseverance in seeking permission from the chief's subordinate for that which his boss had clearly said no.

Daniel gains permission for himself and his comrades to go ten days eating only vegetables and drinking only water: a partial fast to demonstrate the goodness of their God.

Their guard, courageous with trepidation, allows such an experiment to take place. If it works, the diet will be continued; if it fails, the men hopefully will have time to recover what was lost. Either way, the guard will have appeased these young men under his care and gained their respect.

The ten days come to completion, and the guard discovers it was worth the risk. Belteshazzar (Daniel), Shadrach, Meshach, and Abednego now look better and appear healthier than all the other men under his care.

TIME OF REFLECTION

Go Deeper: 1 Peter 2:11–12

We often forget the small steps of *courage of faith* or *submission to fear* we have taken in the past because those choices have led to a pattern of behavior that is now normative in our lives. Take a moment to reflect upon your tendency to choose either courage or caution. What is the source of that tendency?

What has helped you in the past to take steps of courageous faith? What has interfered with your doing so?

Consider these words that might describe the opposite of courage: indecision, faint-heartedness, cowardice, apathy, laziness, or coolness. Can you think of any others?

Someone who has courage can be described as brave, determined, audacious, or backboned. How else might you describe a person with courage?

How is God calling you to flex your courage muscle in a small way right now?

REPUTATION

———— READ PROVERBS 22:1–5, 22–23; PSALM 31 ————

The book of Daniel was originally written in Hebrew (Daniel 1:1–2:4a; 8:1–12:13) and Aramaic (Dan. 2:4b–7:28). The first known and accepted translation of the text to another language was in the Septuagint or Greek translation (a.k.a. LXX). In this translation of the Bible, there is an additional book named after a righteous woman, Susanna. Her story gives us some back history on Daniel.

Susanna and her husband, Joakim, were a wealthy and respected Jewish couple living in Babylon. They sometimes hosted the Jewish judicial council in their home. The story is told that two of the elders sitting as judges in their court each lusted after Susanna. When these elders learned each other's secret, they plotted a way to satisfy their lust.

Together, the elders hid in Joakim and Susanna's garden waiting for her to be alone. When the opportunity arrived, they approached her with this threat: Lie with each of us or else we will testify that we have witnessed you being intimate with someone other than your husband.

The text says that Susanna groaned in response. The weight of the choice made her sick to her stomach. She would not sin by consenting to an extramarital affair, yet to deny their proposal and become a recipient of their false witness surely meant death.

She cried out loud for help, and the two elders yelled in response. Those in the house came rushing to see the commotion, and the elders made their case against Susanna, much to the disbelief of her servants.

The next part of the story is a powerful witness to Susanna's faith and Daniel's wisdom. At court the next day, Susanna's parents, children, and other relatives gathered weeping as they listened to the case presented against her. As she was publicly shamed and given no opportunity for defense, she cried out to God, invoking her Lord to be witness of the truth and the secrets of the elders who accused her.

As they led her out for execution, God stirred the spirit within Daniel's heart, and he shouted, "I want no part in shedding this woman's blood!" (Susanna 45–46 New Revised Standard Version with Apocrypha). He called those present "fools" for not taking the time to fully examine the case. He recognized that false witness had been made against her. In response, the crowd that had gathered invited him to lead the investigation as an elder.

In wisdom, Daniel had each man testify individually and out of earshot of the other. To each, he pointed out their sour character. He recognized the first man as being a dirty judge and the second as having a pattern of sexual misconduct. Separately, he asked, "Under what tree did you see them being intimate with each other?" (Sus. 54, 58 NRSV), to which the two men gave different answers. The gathered assembly recognized each as breaking the ninth commandment to not bear false witness and consequently condemned them to death. Susanna, her family, and the whole assembly praised God for saving the one who placed her hope in Him (Sus. 60).

TIME OF REFLECTION

Go Deeper: Book of Susanna

In this story, we see how a person's reputation and character go before an individual as a witness and as a defense. What type of reputation are you building for yourself?

How are you including God in the building or restoration of your reputation?

What power dynamics do you see at play in this story about Susanna and in what you have read so far from the book of Daniel? What is God's role in the midst of those power dynamics?

WISDOM

——— READ DANIEL 1:17–21; PROVERBS 2 ———

God is the source of all wisdom. The Bible is clear about this fact. In the letter from James, we are told that if any of us lacks wisdom, we should ask God for it because God generously distributes wisdom to all who ask (James 1:5). In Proverbs, we are instructed in wisdom and told that "the fear of the LORD is the beginning of wisdom" (Proverbs 9:10). When offered the opportunity to receive any gift from God that he wanted, Solomon asked for wisdom. 1 Kings records,

> "God gave Solomon wisdom, very great insight, and understanding as vast as the sand on the seashore... He was wiser than anyone... Solomon spoke 3,000 proverbs, and his songs numbered 1,005. He spoke about trees... He also spoke about animals, birds, reptiles, and fish. Emissaries of all peoples, sent by every king on earth who had heard of his wisdom, came to listen to Solomon's wisdom." (1 Kings 4:29, 31a, 32–34)

Even Job in his great grief recognized that "With God are wisdom and strength; he has counsel and understanding" (Job 12:13 NRSV).

After three years of training and preparation, the chief eunuch presented his students to Nebuchadnezzar II. Imagine the anxiety they felt as they waited to be personally interviewed and evaluated by the king. The king tested them thoroughly, and he discovered that four of these students were far wiser than anyone he currently had as his counsel. Wiser than people with far more experience and training. The author of Daniel allows us to know why these four stood out. It was because God had gifted them with wisdom and understanding and had, in particular, given Daniel special insight in understanding visions and dreams. And so, King Nebuchadnezzar invited them to be his attendants, and by doing so, the king unknowingly invited the God of the Hebrews to become his advisor.

The apostle Paul prayed for the readers of his letter to Colossians that they "may be filled with the knowledge of [God's] will in all wisdom and spiritual understanding, so that [they] may walk worthy of the LORD, fully pleasing to him ..." (Colossians 1:9b–10a). We are also recipients of that prayer as we are invited to seek God's wisdom and understanding in all things so that we too might gain spiritual insight.

TIME OF REFLECTION

Go Deeper: 1 Corinthians 1:18–31; Romans 1:16–2:1

The wisdom that Daniel and his companions received from God extended beyond spiritual matters to matters of governing the state. Name one area of your life where you need God's wisdom.

The wisdom of the world or secular wisdom at times looks very different from the wisdom of God or sacred wisdom. What differences between the two have you noticed?

How do you discern what Truth or guidance is coming from God?

An attribute of holy wisdom is humility. Who have you witnessed modeling godly wisdom? How did they express this with humility?

Could someone say of you that you model holy wisdom? Why or why not? Is this something you desire to model? If so, how might you go about gaining such wisdom?

ACTION

Daniel and his friends' world was turned upside down in their youth. Adolescence and our young adult years are transformative regardless of the outside forces that act upon our character formation. Spend some time reflecting upon your teens and twenties and how your character was formed during those years. Write a letter to your younger self. May it be a letter of encouragement offering yourself the words that you needed an adult to speak into your life at that age. What guidance or advice would you have given yourself? Think about how you would have best received these words, and use that language to deliver the message. Then sit with what you have written and invite God to speak to you through it.

DANIEL 2

REVEALER
OF MYSTERIES

DREAMS

For God speaks time and again, but a person may not notice it. In a dream, a vision in the night, when deep sleep comes over people as they slumber on their beds, he uncovers their ears and terrifies them with warnings, in order to turn a person from his actions and suppress the pride of a person" (Job 33:14–17).

God speaks to us in our slumber. Sometimes it is an unnoticed whisper refining and redirecting our soul. At other times, it is vivid imagery that stays with us once we awaken. Not all dreams carry with them spiritual meaning; some are created by our own thoughts, and still others may be the result of a bad diet. But interpretation of dreams belongs to God (Genesis 40:8).

In ancient times, dreams were considered a sound source of knowledge. Today, within public discourse in the United States, they are not given the same credibility as written words, sensory observation, logic, or research. But that doesn't mean God doesn't still speak through dreams. Modern mystics still receive dreams as gifts from God. While others of us may not be as open to this, it does not mean God is not speaking to us.

I have found that when we are too busy to hear God's voice during the day, the silence and stillness of our room at night might afford God the opportunity to be heard. The psalmist writes of receiving instruction and counsel from God while on his bed (Psalm 16:7). He writes of lying awake, searching within his heart (Ps. 4:4), and meditating on God (Ps. 63:6).

God spoke to Nebuchadnezzar II through a dream, and the dream troubled his soul. Dreams can reveal the thoughts of God to people, and for some reason, God chose to reveal to Nebuchadnezzar what was to come.

TIME OF REFLECTION

Go Deeper: 1 Corinthians 2:10–11; 1 Samuel 3

Have you ever had a dream that stuck with you throughout the next day? Do you remember what it was about?

Are you more open to hearing God's voice during the day while you are awake, at night while in bed, or neither? Why?

Have you had a dream recently that you wonder about its meaning? Have you sought God's wisdom for its interpretation?

Keep a journal next to your bed where you can write down any dreams or thoughts that God brings to your mind while you are in bed. Periodically review previously recorded dreams to see if you can find a theme. Record any interpretation.

IMPOSSIBLE TESTS

—— READ DANIEL 2:4–12 ——

There must have been something about this dream that made Nebuchadnezzar II fearful or anxious about its meaning. He needed it to be interpreted, but he set terms for its interpretation that were impossible for any human to meet. Not only was its interpretation to be given, but the dream itself was to be revealed. Nebuchadnezzar didn't trust his advisors to give him an accurate interpretation, so he expected them to reveal the dream without him sharing a hint of it to them. The elements of the dream itself would be kept concealed.

Some would say that Nebuchadnezzar was being a narcissistic, entitled ruler, thinking the impossible was possible and demanding it for himself. Others would say he was being paranoid, suspecting his wise men of purposely misleading him in the interpretation of dreams. Still others might consider him a believer of sorts, recognizing the dream to be of divine origin and thus expecting that a truly wise advisor could acquire of the gods its images and impact.

Nebuchadnezzar had reason to believe that god(s) revealed the future of kingdoms to prophets and that counselors could mislead a ruler when it came to mystic matters. It had happened before. Jeremiah the prophet had proclaimed to the nations that Nebuchadnezzar would rise to power and they were to submit to him. If they submitted, they would survive and their land would flourish; if they did not, they would be exiled and their land would face devastation. Yet Jeremiah also warned these national leaders that their counselors would take this as an opportunity to mislead them. They would deceptively tell them to resist instead of accepting this change in governing power (Jeremiah 27).

There was something about the quality of this dream that made Nebuchadnezzar expect and demand a correct interpretation. And so, he devised a test to evaluate the truthfulness of the interpreter. We will see later that this moment offers an opportunity for Daniel's gift to be revealed to the king, which allows Daniel to be lifted up to a position of influence in the empire. And that will lead to the glorification of God!

TIME OF REFLECTION

Go Deeper: Jeremiah 27; 1 John 4:1–6

Throughout Daniel's story, the magicians, enchanters, and astrologers are shown to be inept when it comes to mystical matters. Only God is able to interpret messages from God. What are some ways that people both inside and outside of the church try to hear God's voice?

In the Old Testament, God's people are warned not to seek the counsel of mediums, spiritists, fortune-tellers, diviners, or the deceased, and not to practice divination, witchcraft, fortune-telling, sorcery, or the interpretation of omens (Leviticus 19:26, 20:6; Deuteronomy 18:9–14; 2 Kings 21:6; Isaiah 8:19). How do you see people doing this today?

In the New Testament, God's people are warned to be wary of philosophy, human tradition (Colossians 2:8–10), and the spirit of deception (1 John 4:6). Instead, the Bible instructs us to "Go to God's instruction and testimony!" (Isa. 8:20a). How are you seeking God's wisdom instead of the world's wisdom?

FACING DEATH

—— READ DANIEL 2:13–18 ——

Have you ever had a time in your life when you faced death, had a close call, or sensed death was all around you? Perhaps it was a devastating diagnosis from a doctor. Or maybe you experienced a near-miss in what could have been a deadly car accident. Or maybe you have people in your life who are unstable and threatening or you live in a place where violence is common. There are times when the Psalmist's words, "My heart races, my strength leaves me, and even the light of my eyes had faded" (Psalm 38:10) ring true to one's soul.

In the book of Daniel, Daniel and his comrades become familiar with the threat of death. It is as if death is chasing them, but God won't let it have its day. In the second chapter, we read of their first recorded run-in with death.

An anxious king who can't find the answers he desires from his advisors exaggerates his problem by pronouncing the destruction of them all. He sends his commander out to literally execute his judgment. And what does Daniel do when death knocks at his door? He doesn't get up in arms to defend himself. He doesn't hide in the corner. He curiously and tactfully interacts with the commander of the king's guard. Daniel inquires, "Why did the king issue such a harsh [urgent] decree?"[1] He investigates to better understand his possible response. Then Daniel acts as if the matter is not yet settled by seeking an audience with the king. It is here that he asks for some time to look for a solution and then solicits his friends to join him in pleading with God for merciful help. Instead of being afraid, Daniel trusts God for the solution.

TIME OF REFLECTION

Go Deeper: Psalm 38; Proverbs 15:1–4; Luke 22:47–52

What is your usual first response when you receive bad news? When you are threatened? When someone near you acts rashly?

What can you learn from Daniel's response that you can apply to your personal life?

In the context of this story, what does pleading for mercy from God look like? (See Jeremiah 33:3.) Is there any place in your life where you need to solicit God's merciful help?

REVEALER OF MYSTERIES

We are invited to worship in wonder the God who is the Revealer of Mysteries. The God whose Spirit hovered over the darkness of the waters at creation (Genesis 1:1–2). Our God who formed us from clay and rib and breathed life in through our nostrils (Gen. 2:7, 21–22). A God who "declared the end from the beginning," saying "my plan will take place, and I will do all my will" (Isaiah 46:10). Our Creator who is so acquainted with us that He knows our thoughts before we even think them (Psalm 139:2), as well as the secrets of our hearts (1 Corinthians 14:25 and Romans 2:16) and yet is generous enough to reveal Divine thoughts to us mere humans (Amos 4:13). For no one "knows the thoughts of God except the Spirit of God" (1 Cor. 2:11) and to those with whom the Spirit reveals them.

For some reason, God chose to reveal his future plans to Nebuchadnezzar and then to confirm the Divine source of those plans by revealing them a second time with the addition of an interpretation to Daniel. It seems that the purpose of the second chapter of Daniel is to make the point that God is the Revealer of Mysteries. It is a significant title and role that is reinforced again and again throughout the book.

TIME OF REFLECTION

Go Deeper: Isaiah 44:6−8; 1 Corinthians 14:20−25

Daniel proclaims that God "reveals the deep and hidden things; he knows what lies in darkness, and light dwells with him."[2] How does it make you feel when you read that God knows and reveals mysteries? Is this comforting or disconcerting? Why?

How does God use this moment to bring Godself glory amongst the Babylonians?

What do both Daniel and Nebuchadnezzar do in response to God's revelation to Daniel?

Do you worship God? If so, how? If not, what holds you back from doing so?

DREAM INTERPRETED

––––––––– READ DANIEL 2:31–43 –––––––––

When a major unexpected event happens, people often look back for signs they missed, warning them of its coming. Often these signs can be found if one looks hard enough. But a retrospective view is very different than a foreshadowing.

Nebuchadnezzar and Daniel have been given foresight into the future through a vision. Daniel acts as an intermediary between God and the king, similarly to how the apostle John acts as our intermediary through the biblical book of Revelation. Daniel relays a dream of a large and bright metallic statue representing the kingdoms to rise after Babylon. This statue is divided into five sections, with each section made of a different quality of metal, the value of each decreasing in expense but increasing in strength as one moves from the top to the near bottom.[3]

The gold head represents the dreamer, Nebuchadnezzar, who rules over what he knows to be the expanse of the world. The silver breast and arms represent an inferior kingdom that is to replace his own. The belly and thighs of bronze represent a third kingdom that will "rule the whole earth." The legs represent a fourth kingdom of strong iron that crushes all others. And a possible fifth kingdom is represented by feet and toes—a divided kingdom of a diverse people, some strong and stable as iron and others brittle as common clay, the two unable to hold together.

Then surprise upon surprise, in the dream, a rock breaks off a mountain and crushes the feet of the statue, causing the entire thing to crumble into pieces and then be blown away. This rock, representing yet another kingdom, then grows into a mountain that takes over the entire earth. Daniel explains that this mountain is the kingdom that will never be destroyed.

Daniel concludes with words reminiscent of the conclusion of Revelation: "This dream is true and the interpretation is trustworthy." At that, Nebuchadnezzar falls in awe and pays tribute to Daniel, just as John fell at the feet of the angel who brought him Revelation. And we are told to "Worship God!" (Revelation 22:6–9 New International Version).

TIME OF REFLECTION

Go Deeper: Revelation 1:1–20, 22:6–9

How does Daniel act as an intermediary between God and Nebuchadnezzar? Has God ever called you to act as an intermediary of faith? How did you respond?

Nebuchadnezzar and Daniel are given a generalized vision of future kingdoms to come. Why do you think God wasn't more specific?

How would you describe this statue and its meaning to someone?

CHAFF

———————— READ DANIEL 2:35; MATTHEW 3:11–12 ————————

How was it that Daniel was able to interpret this dream so easily? Prior to Daniel's lifetime, there were two Jewish kingdoms. The northern kingdom of Israel and the southern kingdom of Judah. You may hear this period in Israel's history defined as "the Divided Kingdom." Isaiah the prophet lived during this time, and he witnessed the fall of the kingdom of Israel and prophesied the fall of Judah, Daniel's home. He also recognized God's judgment of the nations, pronouncing such indictments as, "The nations rage like the rumble of a huge torrent. He rebukes them, and they flee far away, driven before the wind like chaff on the hills and like tumbleweeds before a gale" (Isaiah 17:13) and "The LORD hands nations over to him, and he subdues kings. He makes them like dust with his sword, like wind-driven stubble with his bow" (Isa. 41:2b).

This idea of nations becoming like chaff or dust was not new in the Hebrew mind. Even the Psalmist writes, "The wicked are not like this; instead, they are like chaff that the wind blows away. Therefore, the wicked will not stand up in the judgment, nor sinners in the assembly of the righteous" (Psalm 1:4). In what is likely one of the oldest books of the Bible, Job describes how the wicked are like a lamp put out and like chaff swept away in a storm (Job 21:17–18).

Even John the Baptist, who comes hundreds of years after Daniel, recognizes this metaphor. John prophesies of Jesus, who will baptize with the Holy Spirit, gathering the righteous wheat and burning the wicked chaff (Matthew 3:11–12).

One reason Daniel was able to interpret Nebuchadnezzar's dream once it had been revealed to him was that he was familiar with God's Word. The images matched what he already knew. When he saw the chaff being blown away, he remembered and recalled how this symbolized that the wicked would become no more (Ps. 37:10). The interpretation of this dream was a gift to him and his people, a reminder that God's Kingdom would ultimately reign.

TIME OF REFLECTION

Go Deeper: Psalm 1

How could being familiar with Scripture help you interpret the times in which you live?

How can being familiar with Scripture as a whole help you better understand various passages from Scripture?

How or where do you find hope in knowing that the wicked are like chaff that will be blown away?

MODERN INTERPRETATIONS

—————————— READ DANIEL 2:38–43, 12:8–9 ——————————

A re you still curious about the meaning of Nebuchadnezzar's dream? Perhaps you've attempted to correlate the prophecy about future empires with actual empires that have existed since the time of the Babylonians. Many resources are available to help us understand what we read. In a good study Bible, there are notes that explain the cultural context, make cross-references to other passages of Scripture, list word translation options, and sometimes even deepen our theological understanding. For those who want to go more in depth, there are separate books and online resources called commentaries.

In response to the vision of Daniel 2, for ages people have been trying to figure out which kingdom is which. The ancient writer Jerome, who lived toward the end of the Roman Empire, saw Rome as once being like iron and in the latter days being weak like clay.[4] Without the assistance of scholars, historians, and theologians, when I read Daniel 2, I wonder if the feet could represent modern times: could the iron represent industry, the clay agriculture, and the two together the political tension between these industries and the values of their workers? Or perhaps the feet represent the United States, where people from a variety of ethnic, cultural, and socio-economic backgrounds blend in new ways with each new generation?

How scholars interpret the kingdoms in this vision is often related to how one views prophecy. Is prophecy truth-telling about events current to the prophet's life or is prophecy a foretelling of events to come? For those who see Daniel as a reflective book written in the second century BC, it is more common to interpret the fourth kingdom as Greece. For those who consider Daniel a predictive book written by Daniel in the 500s BC, the third kingdom is correlated with Greece, and the fourth kingdom is interpreted as Rome. Daniel himself interprets the second kingdom as the Medo-Persian Empire (Daniel 5:28).

We will be looking more at modern interpretations of Daniel in future devotions, and this includes coming back to this dream from chapter 2.

TIME OF REFLECTION

Go Deeper: Jeremiah 25:8–14

As you read about the order of kingdoms to come after Nebuchadnezzar's rule, what historical images came to mind? How do you interpret this passage from your contemporary perspective?

When it comes to understanding the Bible, we all have a worldview through which we interpret what we read. What have you been told about the Bible and "true Christianity" that impacts how you understand it?

Are you open to considering different perspectives when it comes to understanding the Bible? Why or why not? If so, are there any boundaries for your openness? What are they? Why?

What does it look like to allow Scripture to speak for itself?

THE FINAL KINGDOM

—————— READ DANIEL 2:44–45; MATTHEW 6:9–13 ——————

"Thy Kingdom come…" Have you heard someone praying these words? These three words are a part of the model for prayer that Jesus gave his disciples when they asked him to show them how to pray. Daily across the world, Christians pray and plead for God's Kingdom to come, for God's will to be done. Yet, many of us Christians don't realize that when we pray these words, we are joining with the Jewish community and their ancient and continual anticipatory prophetic request for the establishment of God's Kingdom or reign on earth.

Early on, this desire was articulated in a hope for Israel to become a great kingdom with a godly ruler like that mandated in Deuteronomy 17. Unfortunately, human rulers are frail and sinful and take advantage of their own people, turning their hearts away from God. When a good ruler comes, his rule is short, as he is mortal. In contrast, God is eternal, a good ruler who delivers His people from bondage into freedom (1 Samuel 8).

When Daniel saw the image in the dream of the stone crushing the iron and clay feet, this image likely brought to mind lyrics from the psalmist—words that created a Messianic expectation for a godly ruler:

> "'I have installed my king
>> on Zion, my holy mountain.'
>> I will declare the Lord's decree.
> He said to me, 'You are my Son;
>> today I have become your Father.
> Ask of me,
>> and I will make the nations your inheritance
>> and the ends of the earth your possession.
> You will break them with an iron scepter;
>> you will shatter them like pottery.'" (Psalm 2:6-9)

Daniel joined with other prophets in declaring that someday God will establish a kingdom that will not be destroyed. The prophet Micah quotes the prophet Isaiah (2:2-3):

> "In the last days
>> the mountain of the Lord's house
>> will be established
>> at the top of the mountains
>> and will be raised above the hills.
> Peoples will stream to it,
>> and many nations will come and say,
> 'Come, let's go up to the mountain of the Lord,
>> to the house of the God of Jacob.
> He will teach us about his ways
>> so we may walk in his paths.'" (Micah 4:1-2a)

As Christians, we see the beginning of the fulfillment of these prophecies in the coming of Jesus as the promised Messiah. Jesus recognized Himself as this Messiah and as a stone. In Matthew, we read:

> "Jesus said to them, 'Have you never read in the Scriptures:
>
> The stone that the builders rejected
>> has become the cornerstone.
> This is what the Lord has done
>> and it is wonderful in our eyes?
>
> Therefore I tell you, the kingdom of God will be taken away from you and given to a people producing its fruit. Whoever falls on this stone will be broken to pieces; but on whomever it falls, it will shatter him.'" (Matthew 21:42–44)

After the resurrection, through the work of the Holy Spirit, the church is established. The church becomes the here and not-yet Kingdom of God on earth. As we read in Revelation 11:15, the full establishment of God's Kingdom is still to come:

> "The seventh angel blew his trumpet, and there were loud voices
> in heaven saying,
>
> 'The kingdom of the world has become
>   the kingdom
> of our Lord and of his Christ,
>   and he will reign forever and ever.'"

In 1 Corinthians 15:24–28, we find further clarification as to what this means:

> "Then comes the end, when he hands over the kingdom to God the
> Father, when he abolishes all rule and all authority and power. For he
> must reign until he puts all his enemies under his feet. The last enemy
> to be abolished is death. For God has put everything under his feet.
> Now when it says 'everything' is put under him, it is obvious that he
> who puts everything under him is the exception. When everything
> is subject to Christ, then the Son himself will also be subject to the
> one who subjected everything to him, so that God may be all in all."

So we pray, "Thy Kingdom come…" knowing our prayer is in the process of being positively answered. God is intentionally working to bring about His Kingdom through Christ and the church.

TIME OF REFLECTION

Go Deeper: Psalm 145; Micah 4:1–8; Zechariah 3:8–9; Isaiah 9:1–7

Have you prayed the words "Thy Kingdom come"? If so, did you think about what that request means?

How would you like to see God's Kingdom come in your life? In the world today?

How do you see God's Kingdom entering the world through the Christian community—the church?

In Nebuchadnezzar's dream, what does the mountain represent? The stone?

How does this vision give Daniel and those in exile hope?

How does this vision give you hope?

GOD-HONORING COMPANIONSHIP

—————————— READ DANIEL 2:46–49 ——————————

They were housemates, classmates, and fellow captives in a foreign land. Together they were a religious community that held each other accountable to the ways of the people of God. Considering the cultural context, it is likely they were also eunuchs, and so Daniel, Hananiah, Mishael, and Azariah formed a much-needed family system of support and friendship.

Although Daniel, for reasons unknown to us, received special favor from God, the other three did not become jealous but instead stood by his side.

When their lives were at stake, Daniel turned to these companions to pray and fast with him for God's revelation. And then when Daniel was lifted up as governor, he used this newfound power to lift them up as well, having them appointed as administrators.

They trusted each other. They had been through a lot together. They needed each other, especially once they were serving the king who destroyed their beloved Temple.

There are at least two types of church:* the local organized church one attends and the Christian community with whom one belongs. Sometimes these are the same, but often they are different. Those fellow believers with whom we live our lives can often be counted on one or both hands. These are the people who celebrate our achievements with us and then take our garbage out when sorrow overwhelms us. These are the people who have earned the right to call us out when we have gone astray. These are the people who regularly pray for us and us for them, as we encourage one another in faith. These are the friendships initiated by God's Holy Spirit, and they are precious and to be cherished.

---

* To name a few other ways of understanding "church," there is also the geographical idea of the global church and the understanding of church as something that connects people across centuries and millennia.

TIME OF REFLECTION

Go Deeper: Romans 12:9–21

Who are your companions of faith?

How do you support one another, encourage each other's spiritual growth, and hold each other accountable?

How is God calling you to care for or show appreciation for them right now?

If you are missing this type of Christian companionship, begin by asking God's Spirit to give you friends like Daniel's friends and to make you a friend like them. Then, if you haven't already joined a Christian small group or a nonprofit or ministry that serves others or does activities together, find one and join it!

ROLE MODELS

W hen life gives you lemons, make lemonade." Both the patriarch Joseph and the prophet Daniel embodied this famous cliché. They were both taken captive to a foreign land and placed as servants under an officer of the king. And God lifted them both up by making them successful, drawing to them the positive attention of those in power.

We can draw a lot of parallels between these two men's lives. They were dreamers and dream interpreters. They continued to follow the restrictive practices of their God and maintained their moral fortitude. God used them to act as intermediaries between God and a nation's leader, allowing the leader to know what was to come so the people could be prepared. And they both faced imprisonment for their holy faithfulness rather than for sin. In each of them, the Spirit of God is recognized.

They were not the same men, though. They each had their own unique trials. They lived in very different time periods. Their familial situations were different. Their life purpose was not the same. Yet, they both chose to live holy lives committed in obedience and faithfulness to God despite trying circumstances. They thrived with God as their help.

Of the many people we are introduced to in the Bible, Joseph and Daniel stand out as role models for generations to come.

TIME OF REFLECTION

Go Deeper: Genesis 37, 39–45, 46–48, 49:22–26, 50

When was the last time you read a biography of someone who overcame challenges to make the world a better place? How did reading their story positively impact you?

Who are your role models? If you don't have any, where can you begin to look to find a role model for yourself?

What can you learn from Joseph and Daniel about how to live a good life despite your circumstances?

ACTION

— RE-READ DANIEL 2 —

Daniel and his friends understood God to be real and accessible. Create a timeline of how you have understood God to be throughout different stages of your life. For example, as a preschooler, you may have believed that God caused the thunder to roll, lightning to flash, and rainbows to decorate the sky. Yet as a teenager, you may have seen God as a moral code you were expected to follow. In your twenties, you may have discovered God to be personal and life-giving. Don't forget to include how you presently view God.

DANIEL 3

MOST HIGH GOD

IDOLS

READ DANIEL 3:1–7

It is almost as if Nebuchadnezzar II (let's just call him "Neb") had ignored Daniel's full interpretation of his dream and centered his attention on the part that stroked his ego—the gold head of a sculpture representing his reign. Perhaps an advisor whispered this focus in worry-filled Neb's mind, telling him not to concern himself with the kingdoms that would overtake his own but to instead focus on the part of the dream that benefited him.

So, he goes and builds a large and striking gold statue, approximately 27 meters high and 2.7 meters wide, in the plains of Dura, Babylon. When it is complete, he organizes a grand symphony of musicians and instruments and then summons every political and government leader in his vast kingdom. He commands the presence of those to whom he has gifted authority, power, prestige, and wealth, many likely indebted to him in some way, if not in fear only. Can you imagine the pomp and circumstance of this state-sponsored occasion? Can you hear the humor in how the author relates these events with lists?

Nebuchadnezzar makes the mistake so many before and after him have made—the setting up of a high place or carved image in place of God. God is not a fan of idols. In fact, God becomes jealous of those persons and things that steal the worship and honor that is due to God. In Psalm 78 we are told how Israel "… enraged [God] with their high places and provoked his jealousy with their carved images" (Psalm 78:58). And it makes sense that this would enrage God that we humans would trade a living, eternal being with actual power for an inanimate, breathless, and destructible image crafted by us (Jeremiah 10:1–16). See the humor in us humans worshipping such an object? In order to protect us from being deceived by such foolishness, God commands us not to create "an idol for yourself in the shape of anything in the heavens above or on the earth below or in the waters under the earth." And to "not bow in worship to them" nor to "serve them" (Deuteronomy

5:8–9). In practical terms, unlike our idols (Jer. 16:19), God is able to promise blessings for us and for thousands of future generations of those who love God and obey God's commands (Exodus 20:6).

TIME OF REFLECTION

Go Deeper: Nehemiah 8, 12:27–47; Isaiah 44:9–25; Revelation 13:14–15

When we think about how people gather and enjoy the idols of our era (entertainment, athletics, education, security, health, progress, and politics), one might wonder why worshippers of God don't assemble in a similar manner. Name some of the ways that people gather to honor that which is not God. How do these contrast with how we gather to worship God? In what ways does the worship of God need to be different? How might it be the same? How might we do a better job of worshipping God? What might that look like?

When the church talks about idols in contemporary times, we often speak of idols symbolically—how people and things gain our attention, praise, and trust and are given priority over and above God. But there are also objects and statues that exist that have gained meaning in such ways that if you were to tear them down, rip them apart, or throw them in the trash, people would be angry. Can you think of an object or a structure that we have built or created that we treat in an idolatrous fashion?

In the local church, division can take place within the community when we hold on to a value, a practice, or an object so tightly that we aren't willing to let it go and trust God with it or our future. How have you seen us make idols in the local church?

THREAT OF A FURNACE

—————— READ DANIEL 3:8–12 ——————

The Chaldeans were a people who came from the area that encompassed the Holy Lands to southern Mesopotamia perhaps three hundred years prior to the events of this story. They were a tribe known for periodically taking advantage of national discord to put one of their own on the throne, as seen in Assyria and then Babylon.[1] Neb's father, Nabopolassar, was one such king.[2]

The ancient writer Chrysostom points out that the Chaldeans would have considered the Jews a threat. He reframes their accusation against the Jewish people, putting the following words in the mouths of the Chaldeans: "These slaves, these captives, who are without a city, you have made rulers over us. But they show contempt for such an honor and treat insolently the one who has given them this honor!"[3] The troublemakers jealously play to their ruler's ego with deadly accusations.

Perhaps you have experienced someone making twisted accusations against you at some point in your life. In a parable recorded in the New Testament, Jesus explains that the devil has sown seeds of weeds in the world, whereas God has sown good seeds. The weeds are those who do evil who walk amongst the good seed, the children of God's Kingdom. They accuse. They cause others to stumble and to sin. They are lawless as they are a law unto themselves (Matthew 13:24–30, 36–43). And Jesus tells us that at the end of the age, at the time of the harvest, the weeds will be thrown into a burning furnace "where there will be weeping and gnashing of teeth" (Matt. 13:42).

Although we may feel the insults of righteous living and the attacks made upon us by accusers who are jealous (Psalm 69), in our times of distress, we are to remember the mighty works of God in the past (Ps. 77) and look forward to our redemption in the future. In today's story, we reflect on how those who sought to see their competition burned alive in a fiery furnace face that same fate as they receive God's judgment.

TIME OF REFLECTION

Go Deeper: Matthew 13:24–30, 34–46

Reading about God's judgment can be both comforting and frightening. What comfort do you gain or what sense of security do you lose when you consider the possibility of the existence of hell?

How have you experienced someone making accusations against you? Were they true? If true, in God's eyes, did the truth of the accusation bring you honor or dishonor? Or if it were false, how does knowing that God knows the truth bring you peace?

Have you ever been an accuser? What do you think motivated you to bring forth the accusations? What might you do differently if you find yourself in a similar situation in the future?

GOD'S POWER VERSUS GOD'S WILL

—————— READ DANIEL 3:13–18 ——————

No matter what happens, I am still God's." These were the words uttered to me over a phone call in which the caller shared that she had found a lump in her breast. When difficult circumstances come our way, sometimes it is hard to know what the faithful response is. Worshipping and trusting God despite the circumstances is always a good response.

Nebuchadnezzar asked the three friends two questions: (1) "Is it true that you don't serve my gods or worship the gold statue I have set up?"[4] and (2) "Who is the god who can rescue you from my power?"[5]

These three young men already have evidence that their God is able to rescue them from this king's rage, as seen in chapter 2. But their faith that God *is able* to rescue them does not lead them to put *God's will* to the test regarding whether God will rescue them again.

The king is not due an answer. In demanding that God rescue the Hebrew men from the furnace to prove God's existence, the king foolishly turns the order of authority upside down. Like a bully, he ignorantly demands action from God, whereas he should instead be humbling himself before the God who gave him the authority to reign.

Nonetheless, the three men profoundly answer his questions in reverse. (2) "If the God we serve exists, then he can rescue us from the furnace of blazing fire, and he can rescue us from the power of you, the king." And (1) "But even if he does not rescue us, we want you as king to know that we will not serve your gods or worship the gold statue you set up."[6]

Shadrach, Meshach, and Abednego give us an example of how we might respond with strength, trust, and submission. Let us join them in saying, "Despite my circumstances, I will still praise You, God!"

TIME OF REFLECTION

Go Deeper: Isaiah 37:14–20; Revelation 7:9–17

The ancient writer Tertullian wrote, "We have a clear ruling to be subject in all obedience … [to] those in authority, but this obedience must be within the bounds of Christian discipline."[7] In reflecting upon the life and writings of Paul, Augustine wrote, "When a choice is offered him of either doing wrong or suffering wrong, he chooses not to do wrong rather than not to suffer wrong."[8] The three friends had to choose between honoring God and honoring their king and between "doing wrong" and "suffering wrong." Have you ever had to make a similar choice? How did it go?

In response to this story, Theodoret of Cyr wrote, "Hence, instead of asking for relief from the troubles unconditionally, we embrace the Lord's planning and providence; and without knowledge of what will be of benefit, we leave the helm to the pilot, no matter what he wishes, understanding clearly that he is able to free us from the threatened evil."[9] How in your life do you need to let go and rely on God's "planning and providence" despite the possible outcome?

DIVINE LIGHT

─────────── READ DANIEL 3:19–27 ───────────

This is a heavy story, and yet there is a lightness in its telling and in its results. If read aloud, the repetition of lists is almost humorous.[10] The way the king is described as his face being distorted with rage is almost a comical portrayal. The sense of urgency and the exaggerated need to use the strongest men to bind up the three Hebrew men almost mocks the excessiveness of the punishment in its retelling. And then there is the abrupt change in the storyline as Nebuchadnezzar notices four men, rather than three, and they are walking unbound in the midst of the flames.

It is at this moment that we must pause and pay close attention, as Nebuchadnezzar observes, "and the fourth looks like a son of [God/the gods]."[11] What is it that Nebuchadnezzar saw that led him to make this statement? What did the fourth man look like? Who is this?

The story unfolds to reveal that this fourth person was an angel sent by God. Angels are "ministering spirits sent out to serve those who are going to inherit salvation" (Hebrews 1:14). At times they are sent to physically deliver God's faithful from harm's way. This is the first appearance of an angel in the book of Daniel. His presence reminds us of the words of the Psalmist, "The angel of the LORD encamps around those who fear him, and rescues them" (Psalm 34:7) and "For he will give his angels orders concerning you, to protect you in all your ways" (Ps. 91:11).

The protection provided in this story was beyond comprehension—not only were the men's bodies and lives preserved but also their clothing. Even the sensory cues that would have told others that they had indeed been in the flames were absent. The excessive nature of the punishment was not enough to undermine the power and preservation of God.

This is a story of the deliverance of those who trust in God. The story reminds us of how Israel was delivered from the iron furnace of Egypt

(Deuteronomy 4:20, 1 Kings 8:51, Jeremiah 11:4). It also foreshadows how the Messiah will deliver humanity from the flames of hell.

TIME OF REFLECTION

Go Deeper: Hebrews 1:7, 14; Isaiah 43

When have you needed God to deliver you? How were you delivered?

Do you think the men in the furnace were aware of the angel's presence? If so, how might this encounter have impacted them?

Have you ever encountered an angel? What happened? How did you know it was an angel sent by God?

RETURN PRAISE!

───── READ 1 KINGS 8:46–53 ─────

I f you survived being thrown into a deadly furnace of fire, what would be your response? Can you imagine the wonder and awe? Would you be humbled that God cared for you that much to save you? Would you break out in praise at the amazingness of God?!

In the Greek Septuagint copy of Daniel, between verse 23 and 24 of chapter 3, there is an addition of two psalms—one from Azariah, a.k.a. Abednego, and the other from the three friends together. In the first psalm, Azariah recognizes God is a just judge: the consequence of Israel's disobedience and sin is banishment to enemy territory. In this prayer, Azariah recognizes himself and his friends as the burnt offering sacrifice for the sins of the people. He also pleads for God's mercy and for their enemies to be deprived of their power.

In the second song, the three men, protected by the presence of an angel amidst the flames, break out in praise of God. Over and over, they call out, "Blessed are you …" They are so wrapped up in praise that they even call on the elements of heaven and earth to "bless the Lord." The song concludes with their recognition that God has saved them from Hades and from death by fire and that God is indeed good.

While Nebuchadnezzar used flames to demand their praise of a human-constructed statue, the three friends instead turned their praise to the more powerful one who could save them from the flames. The words of their praise have been used in worship liturgy throughout the world. As recipients of these prayers, we are invited to seek God's wisdom and understanding in all things so that we, too, might gain spiritual insight into our circumstances and return praise to God.

TIME OF REFLECTION

Go Deeper: The Prayer of Azariah

Have you ever experienced something so awe-inspiring or so freeing that all you could do in response was praise God? Do you remember the details of what happened and why you responded in that way?

The Prayer of Azariah and the Song of the Three Jews are generally recognized as additions to the original text of Daniel, and there is a dispute over whether they should be considered canon (biblical text). The theology of these songs is in line with traditional orthodox biblical theology. Thus, they can be read as liturgy or as religious literature that has benefit for spiritual growth. How have you interacted with non-biblical texts like this that still glorify God?

ABOUT-FACE

READ DANIEL 3:28–30

Have you ever had to make an abrupt about-face? For instance, you announced you were going to do such-and-such, and then you learned some new information that made you realize your plan would not succeed or perhaps it would even cause harm. Then you had to swallow your pride and announce to those involved that you made a mistake.

King Nebuchadnezzar made a dramatic about-face. He went from commanding all the people to bow before a physically tangible gold statue and threatening death if they did not, to recognizing the invisible god of the Hebrew people as the "Most High God" and threatening punishment for those who spoke against this god. He recognized what had just taken place in the faithful witness of these three men and acknowledged it publicly. He even lifted up the fact that they disobeyed his command, and then he rewarded them. Not a typical move for a king!

Imagine how the people must have experienced this. Can you imagine the chatter in the pub or while doing the wash that night or the day after? The God of the Israelites is not only powerful, but this God also cares for and defends His subjects.

God invites us to make a similar about-face in turning toward God from a life of disobedience and disbelief. For some of us, this turning is more dramatic than for others. It may mean taking back words you have spoken in the past or letting go of values that may not be in line with God's will for you. Or perhaps, if you are already a follower, it may mean making a subtle change in your belief system and allowing God to do something new within you. Either way, the invitation stands—the Most High God who delivered Shadrach, Meshach, and Abednego from the blazing fire of the furnace also wants to deliver you and be your God. Are you willing?

TIME OF REFLECTION

Go Deeper: Isaiah 45

How did Nebuchadnezzar's attitude toward God and the three Hebrew men change? Nebuchadnezzar recognized them as "the servants of the Most High God" (Daniel 3:26); what is the significance of this recognition?

How do you respond when a leader makes an about-face? Does it increase or decrease your respect for the person? How does the media's interpretation of the about-face influence your reception of it? What is an appropriate response?

Is God calling you to make an about-face regarding anything in your life?

ACTION

RE-READ DANIEL 3

Reach out to a Christian you know who is a person of faith and ask them to share with you their faith story. Be attentive to how their faith was formed. Was it passed down to them? Did it surprise them suddenly, or did it grow over time? Explore what parts of their story they see as the action or initiative of God and what parts were based on their own initiative or that of another person. How did they respond to God's initiative or action? Some people's faith is born out of or transformed by a time of crisis. Invite the person to share how their faith has changed over the years and if any events impacted it. You may even want to ask how the Christian community or a local church has played a role in their faith story. Ask questions as an interested learner rather than an investigative reporter. Be sure to show respect for the sacredness of the person's faith story. Thank the person for sharing their story with you!

DANIEL 4

KING OF KINGS

SPIRIT OF GOD

—— READ DANIEL 4:1–9, 18, 37 ——

As you read through chapter 4 of Daniel, pay attention to the supernatural element and spiritual dimension of the story: the instructions in the dream are announced by a holy watcher, Nebuchadnezzar refers to Daniel using the name of Neb's god, and a contrast is drawn between the divine and the mortal. Also pay close attention to how Nebuchadnezzar's relationship with God shifts from acknowledging the God of Israel as the God of Daniel to acknowledging this same God as his own.

The Spirit of God within Daniel is a continual witness to the king. Time after time, Divine insight is revealed through Daniel. Neb is very aware of the proximity of relationship that Daniel seems to have with the God of Israel. Neb acknowledges that there is a personal connection that is out of this world.

In a similar way, the Holy Spirit, living within a person of faith, is a witness to that person's colleagues, friends, and family. We are not always aware of how our living by way of the Spirit plants spiritual seeds in another person's journey toward faith, but seeds are being planted. For many, that faith begins by claiming the faith of another, perhaps a parent or a mentor. Then eventually, there comes a time when the person, like Nebuchadnezzar, can no longer lean on someone else's faith but must claim it and live into it as their own. Then they will understand that a relationship with God is available to all who truly fear or revere him (Psalm 25:12–15) and keep his commands (John 14:15–17, 23).

TIME OF REFLECTION

Go Deeper: John 14:15–17, 23

Is your faith your own, or is it a borrowed faith? If it is your own, how did it come to be your own? If it is borrowed, how does reading about the progression of Neb's faith give you insight into your own? Do you believe a different experience of faith or relationship with God is available to you? If so, how?

Would others say that you are filled with the Holy Spirit? What might contribute to them drawing that conclusion?

Do you believe you are filled with God's Spirit? Why or why not?

If you are a follower of Christ, how does knowing God's Spirit is holy and is living within you impact how you live your life?

SYMBOLISM OF TREES

—————————— READ DANIEL 4:10–17 ——————————

Trees are a significant symbol in the Bible and in the ancient Middle East. From Genesis 1 to Revelation 22, we read about how God provides for us through trees and about how people or nations (Ezekiel 31) can be like trees, either fruitful or diseased. We also read of the much-longed-for tree of life and the regrettable consumption of fruit from the tree of the knowledge of good and evil (Genesis 2–3). Even Proverbs symbolically identifies wisdom as a "tree of life" (Proverbs 3:18). In today's passage, we are reminded that trees provide food, shade, and shelter. Trees also add beauty to our landscape (Gen. 2:9), were humanity's original food source (Gen. 2:9), and can be a source for medicinal care (Ezek. 47:12). The power of this symbol has even been captured in the Christian legend of the Three Trees.

In Daniel 4, we read of a tree that symbolizes a person. In Nebuchadnezzar's dream, the watcher refers to the tree as "him" in verse 15, and in verse 16, calls for "his mind [to] be changed from that of a human . . ."

In interpreting the dream, Daniel is likely aware of how, in the past, God used a tree standing strong and bearing rich foliage as representative of either the person who is righteous (Prov. 11:28) or the national leader who is successful (Ezek. 31), and how the tree that is uprooted has represented the wicked, the violent (Psalm 37:35–36), the proud (Ezek. 31:10), and those who trust in their own riches (Prov. 11:28). Thus, he recognizes the act of judgment as the tree is cut down, and the possibility of redemption is found in the remnant of the stump.

TIME OF REFLECTION

Go Deeper: Ezekiel 17, 31

Name several places in the Bible where a tree is used either as a means of God's provision, a symbol, or as a blessing or curse. If you aren't able to do this, take a few moments to either look up "tree" in a biblical concordance or look up "biblical significance of trees" online.

In Jeremiah 17:7–8, we are told, "The person who trusts in the LORD, whose confidence indeed is the LORD, is blessed. He will be like a tree planted by water: it sends its roots out toward a stream, it doesn't fear when heat comes, and its foliage remains green. It will not worry in a year of drought or cease producing fruit." How are you living a life of trust in the LORD?

ALARM

———— READ DANIEL 4:19–27 ————

Daniel heard the message of warning in Neb's dream and was deeply concerned about its meaning. His alarm could be interpreted as selfish self-preservation. Who would want to deliver a message of condemnation to a hot-tempered ruler with a history of lashing out with a death sentence? His alarm could be out of concern for who might rule in Neb's place and how that person might treat the Jewish people living in this foreign land. He also could have felt a sense of righteousness, as justice for the wrongs done to his people was about to be enacted.

But Daniel was a man above reproach who saw the world through spiritual eyes and cared even for the soul of his adversary. He understood that one should feel alarm for anyone facing God's judgment. Daniel also respected the king's title and had been instructed to pursue the well-being of the city in which they now resided (Jeremiah 29:7).

So he announces, "Your Majesty, you are that tree!"

It is interesting how, in this letter, the voice shifts from the first-person perspective of the letter writer to the third-person perspective of a narrator with the telling of the dream's interpretation and its fulfillment. If it is Neb who continues to dictate the letter, it appears he does so from a place of emotional distance. What happens next had to have been traumatic! As the author relates, prior to this moment, Neb "was living serenely in my house, flourishing in my palace" (Daniel 4:1–2a Jewish Study Bible, Tanakh).

And yet, here Daniel explains to him that his great mind would be altered from that of a man to a beast. It would remain that way until he learned to rely upon God's provision, chose to put aside his prideful thoughts, and acknowledged God's sovereign rule even over kings. What a shock to hear that the ruler of Asia, Egypt, and Ethiopia would face such a fate!

Daniel understands that when God says God will do something, God does it (Numbers 23:19; Isaiah 14:24, 27). So Daniel encourages Neb to repent, as there is a biblical precedent for God offering mercy and delaying punishment of those who turn from their sinful ways and humbly turn toward God (1 Kings 21:17–29; Jonah). The Christian theologian Jerome explained that when we repent, the sin is no longer there to be punished.[1] Daniel's guidance for how to repent matches with the early church's understanding that almsgiving or financial charity demonstrates that one has truly changed course.*[2] By being generous, one imitates God's mercy and shows that one is no longer hardhearted toward others, but kind. Daniel is encouraging Neb to stop sinning, to do what is right, and to show kindness to the oppressed. Or as the Proverb states, "The one who conceals his sins will not prosper, but whoever confesses and renounces them will find mercy" (Proverbs 28:13).

---

* See various translations of this passage. "Redeem your sins by beneficence and your iniquities by generosity to the poor; then your serenity may be extended" (Dan. 4:24b JSB, Tanakh). "Break away now from your sins by doing righteousness and from your iniquities by showing mercy to the poor, in case there may be a prolonging of your prosperity" (Dan. 4:27b NASB).

TIME OF REFLECTION

Go Deeper: Book of Jonah

God keeps God's commitments. Read Joshua 21:45, Numbers 23:19, and Isaiah 14:24, 27. How does knowing that God keeps His promises give you hope? How does knowing this serve as a personal warning?

Daniel was alarmed by the fact that Neb was facing God's judgment. He expressed concern for Neb and encouraged him to repent, hoping that in mercy the judgment might pass with no effect. Sometimes we can see what our friends and family members can't see—when they are headed down a path toward destruction. At other times, our friends and family members are the ones who are aware while we are blind to our own course in life. Daniel showed his alarm in verse 19 by expressing the desire for it to impact Neb's enemies rather than Neb. Instead of judging Neb, he desired mercy for him. What can we learn from Daniel's response in feeling alarm for his oppressor? How should we feel alarm for both believers and non-believers facing God's judgment?

In Matthew 19:21, Jesus tells us that if we want to be perfect, we should sell our possessions, give to the poor, and then follow Jesus. This command is often dismissed by Christians as figurative or an extreme. What if we didn't interpret it that way? What would it mean to follow Jesus's directive?

END-TIMES ELEMENTS

─────────────── READ DANIEL 4:23 ───────────────

Apocalyptic texts are in abundance! People expect that since the world has a beginning, it will also have an end. Whether you are an environmentalist or a person of religious faith or both, signs are pointing to the conclusion of the matter—the end of earth as we know it.

Throughout the book of Daniel, we catch glimpses of signs and symbols that warn us of the coming of the end of the age. Even in texts that seem straightforward in their meaning, there is a foreshadowing of something to come. The fourth chapter of Daniel is one such instance.

We read the story of a man who has been the leader of a great empire and who faces punishment for his arrogance until he is willing to humble himself by recognizing the God of Israel as Sovereign. Seems straightforward, and yet, one could wonder if this story offers a parallel outline for what is to come for humanity.

Several foreshadowing symbols can be found in the text. We have the appearance of the watcher, a title that is given to angels in apocalyptic texts.[3] Here the watchers decree judgment upon the great, seemingly global, tree. In cultures around the world and throughout known time, there has been a mythological concept of a "world tree."[4] The tree in this story, while initially symbolizing King Nebuchadnezzar, could potentially also represent the world as a whole.

The year seven is also used to denote the time period in which the king will be humbled. Seven can be purely symbolic as a number that represents completeness, or it can be interpreted literally. It is a number that is frequently used in the prophetic book of Revelation, as it is paired with a number of churches, angels, seals, trumpets, and even stars. Even the time period associated with the number is up for interpretation; it could be pointing to seven years, seasons, half-years,[5] months, or even an indefinite period.[6] The word can even be associated with the rhythm of a woman's hormonal cycle.

And then we have the band of iron and bronze that remains wrapped around the tree stump. It seems as though most scholars have skipped over this symbol in their commentary on the text. And yet, there is a reference to bronze and iron in both Nebuchadnezzar's previous dream, recorded in chapter 2, and in Daniel's upcoming dream, captured in Daniel 7.

So as one reads this chapter, one might wonder if the story itself is a symbol of the future. Does it point to a time when humanity will be humbled and God glorified?

TIME OF REFLECTION

Go Deeper: Revelation 1

What do you think of when you hear the word "apocalypse"?

Have you encountered any symbols or signs that point to the end of the earth as we know it? What are those symbols or signs? How does your faith influence how you respond to these signs? Does it call you to action? A specific attitude? A way of life?

What is the significance of the number seven in the Bible?

THE PUNISHMENT

READ DANIEL 4:24–33, 5:18–21

Twelve months later, it seems as though the terrifying dream and the warning that accompanied it have been forgotten. The punishment arrives just as it was foretold. Nebuchadnezzar arrogantly claims that it is by his own power and his own glory that the kingdom of Babylon was built. He takes all the glory of his kingdom for himself, not attributing any of it to God's doing. The reader is well aware that this is not the case, as even the prophet Jeremiah had prophesied that by the hand of God all nations and even wild animals would serve Neb (Jeremiah 27:6–7). This was the moment in which God inflicted his prophesied judgment and made Neb become like a wild animal eating grass. This is the moment that would serve as a warning to all future rulers to remain humble before the Ultimate Ruler who makes possible their reign (Daniel 5:18–21; Romans 13:1).

God does not have much patience for the arrogance of humans thinking we can achieve greatness on our own. If we look back to the story of the tower of Babel in Genesis 11, we are reminded of how God confused the people's speech, limiting their ability to progress further. This is the event that gave birth to the name Babylon. It seems appropriate then that when the king of Babylon loses his way, God would make him like an animal, stifling his creativity, limiting his ability for complex reasoning, and removing the opportunity to achieve far greater accomplishments, much like how the people at the tower became limited.

Likely to the delight of Judah's exiled, the king who destroyed their Temple* is brought low, even to the point that his nails grow to look like bird claws and his hair to look like feathers. In this imagery, we hear the words

---

* Historically, there isn't any record of King Neb being away from his office, but a story is told similar to this for the last Babylonian king, Nabonidus, who was absent and afflicted for seven to ten years. See: Adele Berlin and Marc Zvi Brettler, Annotations on Daniel 4:1–34, in *The Jewish Study Bible, Jewish Publication Society Tanakh Translation*, page 1649.

of the anguished Job as he responds to his consoler in the midst of his own devastation, "[God] deprives the world's leaders of reason, and makes them wander in a trackless wasteland" (Job 12:24).

TIME OF REFLECTION

Go Deeper: Genesis 11:1–9; Luke 12:13–34

How does pride interfere with our ability to see or acknowledge the truth?

It seems that Neb had forgotten the warning of his frightening dream. In what ways do you keep track of warnings and lessons learned in your life? Can you think of a time you forgot or ignored a warning or repeated a mistake?

Whether we build a tower or build a kingdom, God wants us to remember who ultimately is the source of our success. How do you return the honor to God when you've accomplished something great?

HUMILITY

READ DANIEL 4:1–3, 34a, 36–37

I remember the arrogance of my adolescence. I was an overachiever—that well-rounded student who worked hard to please teachers and parents. If that alone wasn't enough, I was also internally judgmental of others. I couldn't understand why my classmates couldn't get their assignments turned in on time. Then my great-grandmother died. That same week, other troubling events took place, and I was not myself. I yelled at someone at church. I didn't complete my homework. I was even tardy to class, then skipped class due to my inability to control my emotions over being late. And then I realized that it was not fair for me to judge others for the benefits I had received and the detriments life had sent their way. I was not better than anyone else—I had just been given different life circumstances. It was an important and life-changing realization for me to make.

Nebuchadnezzar came to a similar realization when his reason was restored to him after his time in the wilderness. While still recognizing the greatness of his kingdom, he humbly acknowledges the Source of that greatness. He recognizes that God showed justice in inflicting the punishment upon him that God did. Surprisingly, despite Neb's past pride, God gives him even greater recognition in his restoration. After his time lost in the wilderness, his rulers even seek him out.

What is most astonishing is that Neb writes this letter of confession and shares it with his people. This act of vulnerable honesty is admirable and not what one would expect of a domineering world leader. It reflects true humility, as he admits his weakness and glorifies God. He understands that his story is a sign and wonder that brings glory to "the MOST HIGH God." His story is a witness to the people, and his successor King Belshazzar, of how a man who once threatened God's chosen people can now kneel and place his crown before God's throne.

TIME OF REFLECTION

Go Deeper: Psalm 132; Ezekiel 18; 1 Peter 5:5–6

God challenged Job with the impossible: "Adorn yourself with majesty and splendor; and clothe yourself with honor and glory" (Job 40:10). If we are honest with ourselves, we are unable to do this for ourselves. When we've tried, we've likely, knowingly or unknowingly, stumbled. Jesus explained, "Whoever exalts himself will be humbled, and whoever humbles himself will be exalted" (Matthew 23:12). Can you remember a time when you were either unexpectedly humbled or surprised to be exalted? What circumstances led to that situation? Why did it surprise you? What did you learn?

Some have said that many of us are "temporarily able-bodied." Have you ever, like Neb, taken your health or physical and mental abilities for granted? Or have you ever focused so much on your disability or lack of health that you ignored the many other ways God has blessed you with health or ability?

What privileges and challenges do you experience due to the circumstances of your birth or biology? What would it cost you if that were taken away?

GOD IS SOVEREIGN

—————————— READ DANIEL 4:34–35 ——————————

God is ultimately in charge. Sometimes we forget this. We get lost in political and religious debates. We think we can change the fate of humankind. We get a "god complex" and don't even realize we have one.

It is good for us to pause for a moment and reflect on the reality that "the Most High God is ruler over human kingdoms and sets anyone he wants over them" (Daniel 5:21b). As the Psalmist reminds us again and again, God's Kingdom is an everlasting kingdom; God's rule is for all generations. And as a ruler, the LORD is "faithful in all his words and gracious in all his actions" (Psalm 145:13).

In the book of Daniel, you will see this theme repeatedly.

TIME OF REFLECTION

Go Deeper: Psalm 145

"Proclaim the LORD's greatness with me; let us exalt his name together" (Ps. 34:3). How is God calling you to recognize God's greatness and to proclaim it to others?

In Daniel 5:21b, we read that "The Most High God is ruler over human kingdoms and sets anyone he wants over them." How is God either humbling people or glorifying Himself in the kingdoms of which you are a part?

If God is the ultimate Sovereign, as God is unchanging and never dethroned, are you willing to align your life and will toward God's purposes and direction for your life? If so, how do you discern what those purposes and direction might be?

As a society, it appears that we as individuals choose authorities with whom we agree and then accept them as our authorities. We then reject those authorities with whom we disagree. But by doing so, since we choose who we will consider authoritative, are we then making ourselves individually into our own authorities? For authority to be credible, shouldn't it instead receive credentials from somewhere outside of ourselves? If a person or entity is truly deserving of the place of honor given it as an authority, shouldn't there be times in which we disagree but still show respect and consider their authority greater than our own? And are there not also authorities put into place who are not deserving of our full obedience? If this is the case, from whom or from what is authority conferred? And how does one discern when to submit even when one disagrees or when one should revolt against such requests?

Take time to pray for your nation and those who govern you. Recognize that ultimately God is Sovereign over kings, presidents, and even dictators. Then memorize Daniel 4:3.

ACTION

RE-READ DANIEL 4

Practice humility. Take time this next week to humbly serve another person who you wouldn't have thought to serve last week. After completing your act of service, write down who you served and how you hope God was honored by it.

DANIEL 7

(Chapters 5 and 6 have been skipped, but we'll come back to them.)

APOCALYPTIC VISION

A SHIFT IN THE STORY

——— READ DANIEL 6:28–7:1 ———

How does one organize one's own thoughts when presenting them for others to read? Is the goal to entice the reader's interest and build up to the point of excitement, slowly revealing aspects of the characters' personalities and clues as to where the story is going? Or is the goal to present the information in a sequential, straightforward manner? Is it to organize the book by themes or in a stylistic manner?

When we come to the Bible, for a first-time reader, its size alone can be intimidating. Just like an author taking different approaches to organize her thoughts, there are different approaches to reading the Bible. Do you start at the beginning with Genesis and read it straight through to the end of Revelation? Do you select a book within the holy canon that is of interest or has been recommended to you? If this is the case, people often start with a gospel like John or the poetry of Psalms. Some even say a prayer and then open the Bible randomly and read wherever the page may fall open.

Some have found that this random approach helps them come to the Bible with an openness to how God's Spirit may speak to them and an expectation that God will speak. A word of caution: if using this approach, be sure to consider the context of what you read—which biblical book you are reading from and what is taking place before and after the passage.

Daniel is built with two sections, with Daniel 6:28–7:1 marking a shift in presentation. Chapters 1 through 6 record six events that take place in the life of the royal court that include Daniel interpreting the dreams and visions of kings. Some would consider this to be a public historical record. Chapters 7 through 12 detail four apocalyptic visions privately received by Daniel, with Daniel sharing the interpretation of what he has seen. You might say this is written like a private spiritual journal. Within each of these two sections, the stories are presented chronologically, without intermixing Daniel's visions and the visions received by the Gentile kings. This means that although chapters 7 and 8 relay visions that took place prior to King Belshazzar's vision in chapter 5, they are not recorded until after the division in the book, even though they may have impacted Daniel's interpretation and earlier response.

One purpose of this devotional is to make the book of Daniel accessible in bite-size pieces for someone new to reading prophetic literature. Another purpose is to recognize the historical and cultural context in which the visions of Daniel take place. With this in mind, it seems best to approach the visions chronologically, even if that means skipping ahead in chapters and intermixing those received by devout Jewish Daniel with those received by arrogant Gentile rulers.*

As you move forward through this devotional, you'll see this approach, as we skip ahead to chapters 7 and 8 before returning to chapter 5, then waiting to address the famous story of Daniel and the lion's den of chapter 6 until after reading Daniel's prayer, as recorded in chapter 9.

---

* I am choosing to interpret the book of Daniel by recognizing Daniel as a real person who lived and had meaningful encounters with the God of Israel, rather than interpreting him as a fictional character in a narrative that is imagined in order to present a commentary on world events.

TIME OF REFLECTION

Go Deeper: Psalm 19

How does the manner that information is organized impact your ability to receive it? Is it easier for you to understand when things are relayed chronologically? Topically? Imaginatively? Does it help when the logic is straightforward, or is it better when you have to put the pieces together yourself? Do you learn better from parables and fables or from reference materials with places and dates? What does knowing this about yourself tell you about the types of biblical resources (such as commentaries, devotionals, and reference books) that might be the most helpful to you?

How does knowing that others may have a different preference for how information is organized and shared impact how you share information? How does being aware of this help you to be less critical of those who may use a different method of sharing?

The modern printing of the Protestant Christian Bible is divided into two sections: the Old Testament and the New Testament. These sections are then organized by genre—Old Testament: law, history, literature, and prophecy; New Testament: gospels, history, letters, and prophecy. Within each of these genres, the books are organized by chronology, size, or author.

The Jewish or Hebrew Bible, which generally makes up the same books as the Christian Old Testament, although not in the same order or grouping, is organized into three main sections: the Torah or Teaching, the Nevi'im or Prophets, and the Ketuvim or Writings. The combination of the first Hebrew letter of the name of each of these three sections creates the acronym "Tanak(h)," which is the title given to this holy canon. The Prophets are divided into two sections: the former prophets and the latter prophets. Which genre of biblical writing do you find the easiest and most delightful to read?

Which genre of biblical writing challenges you the most? Why?

How do you expose yourself to different types of writing within the biblical narrative?

APOCALYPTIC INTERPRETATION

———— READ DANIEL 7:1–4 ————

I once was told that prophecy can be fulfilled three times, first in the time it was written or shortly thereafter, second in the first coming of the Messiah, and third at the end of days. I will be using this interpretive lens throughout my analysis of the second half of Daniel. In apocalyptic* biblical prophecy, Babylon becomes a symbol of not only the enemy of Israel at the time of its writing but also of Rome during the time of and time after the incarnational witness of Jesus the Messiah, and later of a final great conquering nation. In all three, we see God rise to eventually thwart the nation's leader's evil ways, revealing the power of God in His kingdom and saints (Isaiah 13–14). In today's reading, Daniel receives a vision of four great beasts representing four kingdoms on earth. These four kingdoms will eventually be replaced with an eternally forward-moving kingdom made of God's saints.

Keep in mind that when interpreting symbolic apocalyptic text, it can be easy to inappropriately correlate the symbols with current events and people, as these are the things we are most familiar with and aware of. For example, as of this writing†, the United States has just completed its withdrawal of military forces from Afghanistan after twenty years of presence. Within the last few days, the world has watched in surprise as the Taliban has swiftly moved in and taken control. Since my attention is currently focused on the seventh chapter of Daniel, I naturally see the beginning of its fulfillment in these events, whether or not the events truly align, with Afghanistan being represented by the symbols of the first beast, the one with a lion's head and eagle's wings that eventually rises to stand like a man.

For the Afghan people, a lion named Marjan held in captivity at their zoo

---

* Apocalyptic means "unveiling the hidden."

† The morning of August 17, 2021.

became a symbol of their will to survive. This lion fought to defend his mate from an attack by a soldier and was significantly maimed in the process. Marjan became a national symbolic hero. He died of old age around the time the United States, symbolized by eagle's wings, began its occupation, yet his symbolic power has remained in the narrative of the people. The image of the lion's head with the eagle's wings, which are suddenly ripped off, aligns with the sentiment of US observers of current events, a sense that "we've" torn off the wings to fly, to "be free," away from the Afghan people. We are waiting with trepidation to see if the result of this moment is the Afghan nation being set up on its own two feet and given a "human mind," or if it will backslide into a time of darkness and oppression.*

It is a human tendency to interpret prophetic text from the lens of the time within which we live. As we interpret the seventh chapter of Daniel, we need to keep in mind that this is taking place during the "first year of King Belshazzar of Babylon," likely around the 550s BC,[1] with the events likely being recorded and shared at a later date, some argue around the time of Antiochus Epiphanes in the 100s BC. Keep this in mind as we continue forward.

---

* Again, this is from a US perspective in the fall of 2021.

TIME OF REFLECTION

Go Deeper: Isaiah 13:1–14:23

How have you typically responded to prophecy or future foretelling? Is this of interest to you? If so, what aspects of it draw your curiosity?

How familiar are you with biblical prophetic and apocalyptic texts? If you are familiar, who has influenced your interpretation of them?

What is your current sentiment toward these types of sacred texts? Why? What informs this sentiment? Are you willing to consider other perspectives? Why or why not?

THE FIRST THREE BEASTS

Before God spoke, "Let there be light," there was darkness and the Spirit of God moved over the deep waters (Genesis 1:1–3). As we prepare to hear of a new creation,[2] we once again find ourselves watching the water. The breath of God that breathes life into dead bones and promises a return from exile (Ezekiel 37:9–14) stirs the great sea. Or as Greek mythology emphasizes, seasons change with weather-altering cardinal winds.[3] A new season of humanity is about to come to pass but not without first passing through rough waters. This symbolic sea has been generally recognized as representing the whole world[4, 5] or all of life[6] (Matthew 13:47). We read in chapter 7 of the stirring of the world. But to some, like St. Augustine, the only ones who are stirred are the "people filled with bitterness" and not the "devoted souls."[7]

From this foaming sea suddenly emerge four aggressive beasts. We are told explicitly that these "beasts" each represent one of four kings or kingdoms. Each beast is described as a combination of several living creatures. Yet when we enfold the characteristics of all four into one, we get the image of the worshipped, wounded beast who has a global human following as described in Revelation 13. As written here, one can wonder if these four kingdoms occur sequentially, with one beginning sometime after a previous one ends; simultaneously, with all ruling at the same time, but perhaps in different geographic regions; or if they appear chronologically but reign concurrently. Do they span the entirety of history, or are they four kingdoms that emerge quickly in a row at the end? Could there be gaps of kingdoms unmentioned in between?

In verse 11, we hear of the destruction of the fourth beast (likely representing a caliphate/nation-state/empire/league), and verse 12 reads, "As for the rest of the beasts, their dominion was removed, but an extension of life was granted to them for a certain period of time."[8] This leads us to believe that at the end, they coexist. Who are these beasts? It is assumed that the symbolism of these four beasts adds further understanding to Nebuchadnezzar's vision of the statue, which also represented four kingdoms, as described in Daniel chapter 2.

Most commentators interpret these beasts historically, with the first beast (the head of gold in Nebuchadnezzar's vision) representing Babylon. As evidence of this interpretation, reference is often made to how the prophet Ezekiel, a contemporary of Daniel, received a word from God (Ezek. 17:1–18) that used the image of an eagle to represent two nations. Within that vision, it was revealed that the eagle first symbolically represented the king of Babylon[9] and then later the pharaoh of Egypt.[10]

The theologian and historian Jerome recognized the eagle's rank among birds as equal to that of the lion among animals.[11] One has to wonder about the symbolism of joining together the body of the lioness with the wings of an eagle, the removal of these wings, and the resulting emergence of a biped with a human mind. What do the removal of these wings and this transition imply about this king or kingdom that has been or is still yet to be? Could this be another way of telling the story of the time when King Neb was humbled in the wilderness and then restored to regality?

If we want to leave room for a more contemporary analysis of these creatures, we can consider the national animals or emblems that exist today that correlate with the symbolism contained in this chapter. Many nations have chosen the lion to represent their national strength. Fewer, but as many as nineteen, have selected the eagle as a national emblem.[12,13] The Burmese use the glamorized chinthe and mythical manussiha as religious sculptures. Could some new nation other than Babylon be represented by this first beast?

The second beast, the rib-gnawing, flesh-consuming bear, is treated as a parallel revelation to the statue's silver chest and arms of chapter 2.* It is often associated with the Persian Empire,[14] sometimes with the Median Empire,[15] and at other times a combination of the two. Theodoret of Cyr wrote about how savage or torturous the Persians were in how they treated those they captured,[16] which brings to mind the image of the three ribs between the bear's teeth. The meaning of the three ribs is up for discussion. They could

---

* See the devotional from Day 12.

represent three nations, such as the Medes, Assyrians, and Babylonians,[17] three regions,[18] three language-groups, or even three sub-rulers, such as Daniel and his two counterparts governing under King Darius (Daniel 6:1-2).

The Medo-Persian Empire covered a belt of land from north Africa to India,[19] or the three ribs of Lydia, Babylon, and Egypt.[20] The progeny of this empire would be the Iranian people. Russia* is the only country that currently uses the bear to represent itself, although Finland has recognized the brown bear as its national animal.[21]

The third king and kingdom has frequently been associated with the kingdom of bronze that ruled the whole earth in Daniel 2:39 and identified as Alexander the Great and the Macedonian/Greek/Persian kingdom he ruled. The speed of the leopard and the four heads of this creature remind historians of Alexander's speed and his four generals: Ptolemy, Seleucus, Antigonus, and Cassander (Antipater) or Alexander's brother Philip.[22] Others have identified this beast with the Persian Empire, subsequently recognizing the fourth beast with ten horns as representing Alexander's Greek Empire and his ten Seleucid successors.[23] While in modern times, many countries have a bird as the national symbol, only five countries have chosen a leopard as the national emblem: Benin, Democratic Republic of Congo, Republic of Congo, Denmark, and Somalia.[24] Other spotted felines recognized as national animals include the jaguar (Guyana, Mexico), ocelot (Mexico), snow leopard (Pakistan), and lynx (Romania, Serbia).[25]

---

* Note: This devotional was written prior to Russia's attack on Ukraine that began in 2022.

TIME OF REFLECTION

Go Deeper: Genesis 1:1–5; Hebrews 12:1–15, 25–29

A professor of Hebrew Scriptures, André LaCocque, argued that "Daniel's synopsis divides human time into four successive periods of decline. Humanity as a whole (not just Israel) is regressing toward a historical point very much in the image of the initial chaos, before God created the cosmos."[26] Do you agree or disagree with the professor's interpretation of Daniel? Do you think that the Bible predicted global decline?

Have you ever experienced a tumultuous time in life that led to a time of peace? If so, what was it like during the rough seas of that stage of your life? Then what was it like when you reached a season of peace? If you haven't experienced this, how have you observed someone else going through such a season of life, and what did you learn from them?

Considering the different animals associated with present-day nations, do you see any correlation between this text and present-day circumstances? Is it being fulfilled in any way today?

THE FOURTH
BEAST WITH HORNS

—————————— READ DANIEL 7:7–8, 19–20, 23–24 ——————————

M any people, while familiar with popular culture depictions of an apocalypse, are not familiar with biblical apocalyptic text. When read initially, these texts appear confusing and mysterious. Yet, as one reads more and more of these texts, one quickly discovers that the same message is repeated using different illustrations and symbolism. As you read through Daniel 7, it may seem confusing. Yet, when we read it in comparison to Daniel 2, Revelations 12–13, and Revelations 17, we become aware that this is a progressing message that God has revealed more than once so that we might have some level of expectation about what is to come. While the details remain mysterious, the building blocks of events gain clarity with the passing of time.

The fourth beast is the most terrifying of them all. It has iron teeth and bronze claws. It represents a fourth king or kingdom that "will devour the whole earth, trampling it down and crushing it."[27] Like the feet of Nebuchadnezzar's statue, this fourth beast tramples what is "underfoot." The imagery of devouring, trampling, and crushing is repeated for emphasis. How are we to understand this world dominion? Is this done through war? Harm to the environment? Consumption and greed? Psychological manipulation? Culture and media? We can hear the beginning of the reverberation that is later felt in Revelation when a great martyrdom takes place.

This kingdom will be unique; it will be unlike the others that came before. Take note that, unlike the first three beasts, this beast is not likened to any animal. One distinguishing feature is the set of ten horns on its head. We see these ten horns mirrored in both the dragon and beast mentioned in John's apocalyptic letter of Revelation (12:3, 13:1, 17:12). We also hear a reflection of the unnumbered, but assumed at ten, toes of Daniel chapter 2. These toes were a mix of iron and clay, representing a divided kingdom with a mixture of people who can't stay united.[28]

In the Bible, a "horn" represents a ruler (see Psalm 148:14 for one of the more positive examples of this use.) If reading this prophecy during the time of the Maccabees, one might interpret this to be a commentary on the Macedonians or Greeks and the ten Seleucid rulers following Alexander the Great, which would include Antiochus,[29] or ten successive kingdoms leading up to Antiochus Epiphanes.*[30] If reading this in the early Christian church, we might expect ten kingdoms to emerge from the militaristic "bronze claw"[31] of the Roman Empire.[32] Those reading soon after the fall of Rome might interpret this as predicting a future rebirth of the Roman Empire.[33]

Modern interpreters might compare these ten to an Arabian confederacy, the former British Empire, or a European Union, and they may even ask, "How many dominant empires have there been since Rome?"† Do we interpret them to be ten sequential rulers or ten rulers ruling simultaneously in some sort of confederacy? Revelation 17 tells us of ten kings who will each receive authority and power for an hour for the sole purpose of diverting and amassing it to be then given to one tyrant.[34] Could these ten rulers be the same as the ten alluded to by this imagery of the horns?

Who the fourth kingdom is interpreted to be evolves with history. Whether it is Macedonia, Rome, Nazi Germany, a state that currently exists in our geopolitical world, or a kingdom yet to come, we must keep in mind while reading that while this kingdom has a global impact, it will place a heavy weight on Israel, as Israel is the first audience of this prophetic book. We may choose to find encouragement from reading about this fourth kingdom, knowing that even though it is terrifying, it will come to an end and be replaced by the Kingdom of God. Dr. André LaCocque in the *Global Bible Commentary* emphasizes this as revolutionary good news for the oppressed.[35] In fact, in Revelation 19:20, we read of this fourth beast being thrown into the lake of fire. Although it will prevail for a while, its time will come to an end. God will have the victory!

---

* Jerome references Porphyry of Tyre's "Against the Christians," in which he sees the ten horns as ten successive kingdoms leading up to Antiochus Epiphanes. Unfortunately, we no longer have copies of this work by Porphyry.

† If desiring to work out that math in a contemporary fashion, here are some empires that might be counted: Umyyad Caliphate, Mongol, Ottoman, Spanish, French, Russian, British, and the United States.

TIME OF REFLECTION

Go Deeper: Revelation 13

The four kingdoms serve to remind us that all kingdoms will be stripped of their authority and will eventually pass away, except God's Kingdom. We tend to forget this. What makes it either easy or hard to believe that someday your nation will no longer stand with authority? Is it easy or difficult to trust that this will happen in God's timing? How does it make you feel to consider this reality?

Isaiah 45:2–3 states, "I will go before you and will level the mountains; I will break down gates of bronze and cut through bars of iron. I will give you the treasures of darkness, riches stored in secret places, so that you may know that I am the LORD, the God of Israel, who summons you by name" (NIV). These words of Isaiah are addressed to Cyrus. How do you understand God's involvement in political affairs? How does your understanding compare with the scriptural examples of God's relationship with government? Do they agree or disagree, and why?

THE MACCABEES

———————— OPTIONAL READING: 1 AND 2 MACCABEES ————————

C ould it be that the four kingdoms referred to in Daniel have already taken place? Could it be that these prophecies were fulfilled in the time between the final events of the Old Testament and the establishment of the church in the New Testament? This time period is known as the Intertestamental time period, and it includes four eras: Persian Era (432–330 BC), Hellenistic Era (330–167 BC—think Alexander the Great), Hasmonean Dynasty (167–63 BC), and the Roman Era (began in 63 BC).[36] These four "kingdoms" transition us from the time of the kingdom of Israel to the time of Jesus preaching, "Repent, because the kingdom of heaven has come near" (Matthew 4:17).

When reading commentaries on the book of Daniel, references are often made to king Antiochus IV Epiphanes (175 BC[37] or 168/167–164 BC[38]) who tried to "enlighten" the Jewish people with Hellenistic ideas by massacring them[39] (1 Maccabees 1:54–61) and desecrating the Temple in Jerusalem by removing the sacred objects and offering offensive sacrifices (1 Macc. 1:41–50). You'll also hear references to the Messianic or priestly-king figures who led the Jewish revolts, defending the Jewish people and their religious practices: Judas Maccabeus and the descendants of his father, and the priest Mattathias (a.k.a. the Hasmonean family). This family stood up for holiness and militaristically fought against cultural indoctrination, heavy tributes, and the intentional dilution of their religious community and faith. Judas Maccabeus was seen as a Messianic figure, one who fulfills the Messianic promise and brings about the Kingdom of God.[40] The terror of Antiochus IV Epiphanes and the freedom-fighting of the Hasmoneans are recorded in both 1 and 2 Maccabees, the source of reference for many of these commentaries.

It is in the context of the time after the Maccabees that Jesus arrives on the scene. His leadership stands in contrast to the people's expectation of another Hasmonean Messianic-like militaristic ruler. Unlike his predecessors, Jesus brings about a "peaceable," although divisive, kingdom (Isaiah 11:1–9

and Luke 12:53). His influence is divine and is expressed through both compassion and subversion. He speaks of the Kingdom of God and people being
led by the Spirit, in contrast to the kingdoms of this earth and being led by
legalism. He speaks of God, not man, being the ruler. He reestablishes the
God-centeredness of God's kingdom in Israel and shows the way for Gentiles to become a part of it as well.

Reading 1 and 2 Maccabees adds an understanding of context to our reading of the New Testament and, for some interpreters, clarity to the reading of
the book of Daniel. 1 and 2 Maccabees can be found in the Roman Catholic and Orthodox Deuterocanon, which Protestant Christians refer to as the
Apocrypha. It is also within 1 Maccabees where we find a record of the historical events celebrated at Hanukkah.[41] If you are a reader who enjoys history, you may also find the work of the historian Josephus of interest.

TIME OF REFLECTION

Go Deeper: Matthew 5

The book of Daniel has been considered a book of subversive resistance and was banned by the Japanese during WWI and hidden by the rabbis during the rule of Rome.[42] How do books like Daniel and 1 and 2 Maccabees strengthen people who are oppressed?

How was Daniel's resistance different than that of the Jewish community under the leadership of the Hasmoneans? Which form do you prefer and why?

What is subversive about the message of Jesus? If you need help considering this question, check out his sermon recorded in Matthew 5.

THE ARROGANT LITTLE HORN

──────────── READ DANIEL 7:8, 11, 20–21, 24–25 ────────────

What are the characteristic traits of the anti-Christ? The little horn of Daniel 7 has been described as one with human eyes and an arrogant mouth. Arrogant enough to speak against the Most High. You will recognize this individual as one who wages war against and oppresses or wears out the holy ones and prevails for a little while but is eventually destroyed. You will see in this ruler an intent to change laws as well as the times.

Recognize the setup for this antagonistic ruler. The fourth beast has ten horns. This means that ten rulers will arise from the fourth kingdom. This ruler will emerge either from among or, more likely, after these ten and will supplant three of them in his rise to prominence.

Keep in mind that this little horn is also described as looking "big." Theodoret of Cyr explains that this means the ruler comes from a small nation like Israel but becomes great by ruling over three provinces instead of one like the other seven horns.[43] Ancient Christian commentators like Jerome[44] and Hippolytus[45] expected this little horn to overthrow Egypt, Libya, and Ethiopia.[46] Some have compared these three to the First Triumvirate of Rome (Pompey, Crassus, and Caesar) and their disregard for the Jewish religion. There is a general expectation built upon associating this little horn with the beast of Revelation 13—that this ruler could expect to receive the worship of all people. Paul, Silvanus (Silas), and Timothy, in their second New Testament letter to Thessalonica, write, "He opposes and exalts himself above every so-called god or object of worship, so that he sits in God's temple, proclaiming that he himself is God." They describe this man as the "man of lawlessness" who is "doomed to destruction," and he comes at a time of "strong delusion" that allows for people to believe this authority's "false miracles, signs, and wonders" (2 Thessalonians 2:3–4, 9, 11).

Based on what we've read so far in Daniel, we can expect the arrogance or pride of this individual to become the place upon which God's gavel descends.

TIME OF REFLECTION

Go Deeper: Psalm 12; 2 Thessalonians 2

For those living in a nation-state with true religious freedom, the threat of martyrdom may feel distant. But for others, it is never distant. Life-threatening religious persecution continues to take place around the world. A martyr is a person who is killed because of their beliefs. How familiar are you with the stories of those martyred in recent years?

How far are you willing to go to defend your religious faith?

What beliefs of yours are worth dying for? What beliefs are not?

If you shared your answer to the last question with a trusted friend or your family members, would they say they support your willingness to die for those beliefs, or would they question your allegiances and commitments?

What value is there in protecting religious freedom? Whose religious freedom should be protected?

Take a moment to invite God to give you wisdom and to form your faith according to God's purposes and will.

TIME, TIMES, AND HALF A TIME

—————————— READ DANIEL 7:25 ——————————

I grew up a child of the 1980s and early 1990s. I grew up in the middle of the United States, and this was a time when fictional apocalyptic religious literature was popular among the circles of adults I interacted with. Books like Paul Meier's *The Third Millennium* and Tim LaHaye and Jerry B. Jenkin's bestselling *Left Behind Series* graced our shelves. Then in the late 1990s, my parents and I began traveling the country, visiting college campuses to discover where I would go to school. Since the year 2000 was approaching and there was fear that computers would not be able to handle the digital transition from the 1900s to 2000s, at each stop, my parents would ask, "Has the school prepared its computer technology for the possible Y2K glitch?" The future felt foreboding.

It was in this 1980s to 1990s cultural context that I heard interpretation after interpretation of what "time, times, and half a time" meant. To my young ears, the exact length of an expected time of tribulation for the earth and its inhabitants was clearly marked. Unbeknownst to my younger self, the rest of the verse explicitly states this will be a difficult time specifically for "the holy ones." So, this single verse stood out in my mind as I came to write this devotional.

Now, as an adult, when I read this passage, it stands out to me that the passage begins by stating that this evil ruler will "intend to change religious festivals, and laws,"[47] or as otherwise translated, "try to change the set times and the laws."[48] I wonder if this means that how people talk about time may change prior to this "time, times, and half a time." Could the word "time" become a specific form of measurement? Kind of like how we measure an "hour" or a "minute"? Perhaps "time" will come to mean something that it didn't mean when this verse was originally recorded or doesn't mean in the present moment. I've wondered, "Could a 'time' refer to a term of office or some other unit of measurement?" Or perhaps it could refer to different eras. For example, in the United States, we think of the time between the bombing of Pearl Harbor and the events of 9/11, and then we think of the time between the events of 9/11 and the global COVID-19 pandemic.

It seems clear, though, that there will be a period of time, then a second period that is longer, and finally a third that is much shorter than the second and half the time of the first. The most common interpretation is the one proposed by the ancient biblical translator Jerome, who recognizes the Hebrew word for "time" in this verse as literally "one year." So "times" is double that at "two years," and "half a time" is half a year. Which means we come to three and a half years.[49] We then must ask, "Whose calculation of a year?" As this book is credited to a Hebrew writer and addressed first to the Hebrew people, the natural interpretation is to use the Hebrew calendar year.

Earlier in Daniel, we read that God is the one who "changes times and seasons" (Daniel 2:21). So even if a human ruler attempts to change things, God in God's sovereignty gets to define them. As we encounter Scripture that defines time frames and people begin to speculate on meaning, we must remember that ultimately God is the book's author and the arbitrator of interpretation whose authority governs the actual timeline.

TIME OF REFLECTION

Go Deeper: Revelation 12

I received my first full English translation of the Bible when I was in third grade. I think I had read through it entirely by fourth grade. In my first reading, I took everything literally. Since then, I've discovered other interpretive lenses, such as allegorical, spiritual, historical, and narrative. How do you imagine a child interprets Scripture compared to an adult? How about someone in their twilight years? At what age did you first encounter Scripture? How has this influenced how you interpret it?

How does our childhood religious experience influence our present-day understanding of Scripture and its meaning?

Think of a time when you realized a childhood memory was inaccurate due to your thinking like a child and not seeing things from an adult perspective. Consider how some of your religious beliefs may have been inaccurately informed in a similar manner. Knowing this, how can we be open to reading Scripture as if for the first time when re-encountering biblical stories that we first heard in our youth?

ACTION

──────── BREATHE ────────

Take a moment to breathe. The past several days' readings have been quite heavy. But when we return to Daniel 7 tomorrow, we will be reading the verses that speak of God's glory! Soon after that, we'll be reading about the good news! But for now, let's rest for a moment. Jesus said that the "Sabbath was made for man, not man for the Sabbath" (Mark 2:27 NIV). Although today may not be the Sabbath, take a moment to recognize God's presence. Go for a walk in nature. Find a silent place to retreat for twenty minutes. Bake bread. Ask permission to sit in the silence of an empty church sanctuary. Read your favorite Bible story. Pray. Take a moment to breathe and recognize the gift of God's presence.

ANCIENT OF DAYS –
THE LORD GOD

—————————— READ DANIEL 7:9–10 ——————————

The wrath of God is not a topic we like to talk about, yet here in Daniel 7, its voice announces itself quite loudly and *beautifully*. We read an awe-inspiring scene filled with images that are otherworldly: the Ancient One appearing in glory in a time that heralds our ultimate future, the "renewal of all things" (Matthew 19:28 NIV). Thrones are being set up. The Ancient of Days takes His seat. He is surrounded by His royal court, and an innumerable number of beings attend to Him. This is a powerful image symbolically pointing to God, the Father Creator. Let's look at this imaginative, poetic interlude in further detail.

We begin with a reference to this ancient presence, of one whose being points back in time without a real sense of aging: the eternal being. The idea of ancient also carries with it a biblical understanding of a past and ongoing wisdom being called forth into this future moment.

The descriptor "white" followed by images of flowing flames bring light and vibrancy into this scene. It is important that we understand that "white" is the color of the radiance of light. This isn't "white" as in how "white" or "black" are used to refer to skin color, which is quite inaccurate, but more like the white of snow reflecting the light of heaven. This is how light penetrates the darkness, making that which is hidden, hidden no more. It is like how truth cuts through and delivers us from shame and how forgiveness releases us of the burden of guilt. The image we are to receive here is of One who is blameless and holy. This is a figure radiating light and carried by flames. In other places, this Ancient One is depicted as surrounded by colorful light like that of a rainbow (Ezekiel 1:27–28; Revelation 4:3).

We read of clothing and hair, yet the anthropomorphism or descriptive embodiment of God here is likely symbolic. Chrysostom points out that God the Eternal Father has no need for clothes, hair, or a physical throne.[50]

The Psalmists write of a devouring fire (Psalm 50:1–5) that goes before God consuming God's foes (Ps. 97:3). In the way Isaiah writes of God's breath and voice, one can liken it to a fire-breathing dragon speaking judgment on the nations while simultaneously pouring life-giving rain upon Zion (Isaiah 30:19–33). In Zephaniah, the fire of God's jealousy consumes the earth (Zephaniah 1:18), and in Hebrews, we are told, "for our God is a consuming fire" (Hebrews 12:29). Malachi writes of God's fire as purifying and compares it to a professional washer's soap. With it, God will purify the religious leaders who will then bring righteous offerings on behalf of the people (Malachi 3:2–4).

And although our attention is focused upon the glory of this One set before us, as we read these verses, we also become aware of the hundred million people gathered around this divine entity. Their presence seems to add to the Ancient's singular greatness in contrast to their individual anonymity.

This imagery calls the reader to take a moment to recognize how awe-inspiring this scene is—and to meditate upon the holiness and awesomeness of God.

> "The Mighty One, God, the LORD,
>   speaks and summons the earth
>   from the rising of the sun to the
>   place where it sets.
>   From Zion, perfect in beauty,
>   God shines forth.
>   Our God comes and will not be silent;
>   a fire devours before him,
>   and around him a tempest rages.
>   He summons the heavens above,
>   and the earth, that he may judge his people:
>   'Gather to me my consecrated ones,
>   Who made a covenant with me by sacrifice.'
>   And the heavens proclaim his righteousness,
>   For God himself is judge.
>   Selah"
>   (Ps. 50:1–5 NIV)

TIME OF REFLECTION

Go Deeper: Revelation 1:12–17, 4:1–11

Sometimes in adulthood, our imagination is stifled. Yet, as we read passages of Scripture that speak of a time yet to come or the spiritual realm, the ability to imagine and picture the unbelievable is beneficial. Where in your life do you have the freedom to let your imagination express (exercise) itself? Where in your life is your imagination stifled? How might exercising one's imagination be beneficial in faith formation and the receptivity to God's voice?

A plethora of beings serve God. We don't know for certain what type of beings they are. Are the thousands upon thousands human? Are they angelic? A mix of both? Perhaps animals and even life of which we are unaware join in the multitude. Let's choose for the moment to interpret this text as referring to humans. Imagine yourself in a crowd of one hundred million people who are all focused on serving God. How might that impact your understanding of yourself? Others? Christianity? God?

Now imagine that the multitudes serving God are angels. How does that impact your view of the world?

JUSTICE

READ DANIEL 7:11–12, 21–22, 26–27

As I reflected upon this chapter, I experienced a growing anticipation for the end of days and the establishment of God's Kingdom. I began to embrace the hope found in the destruction of the beast and the little horn—a victory to be celebrated! But then naturally, I also had to wrestle with the burden of this idea that those guided by human flesh will also meet destruction. This is a story of justice—of victory, destruction, and re-creation. Justice has that characteristic: judgment brings punishment upon the guilty* and release for those who are justified. Yet, we all know that at times in our lives, we have been deserving of the heavy hand of justice and felt a deep longing for mercy. Sometimes we have been lucky enough to receive an embrace in response to our cries for mercy. At other times, we have been the person responding with the gift of mercy and forgiveness. As either a recipient or giver of mercy, we have experienced the power of forgiveness and re-creation.

Daniel 7 recognizes the victor, God; the condemned, the beast, and those who live guided by the flesh; and the honored, those whose names are written in the book of life who will be blessed to be partakers of God's Kingdom. In this chapter, we learn that not only will God be the judge but also those seated in God's court will judge. In the New Testament, Jesus says, "When the Son of Man sits on his glorious throne, you who have followed me will also sit on twelve thrones, judging the twelve tribes of Israel" (Matthew 19:28 NIV). In Revelation 4, we read of twenty-four elders on thrones—perhaps this includes both the twelve apostles and the leaders of the twelve tribes of Israel. And the writer of 1 Corinthians asks, "Do you not know that the saints will judge the world?" (1 Corinthians 6:2a NIV).

---

* Generally, in non-end-times life, the hope is that the punishment will bring about a change of heart and a change of direction, both for the offending party and for those who are supportive of the offense. The desired result is that even the guilty will end up finding release from the weight of their sin through their repentance. But the context of today's reading is the end times, when the opportunity for repentance has passed.

In Revelation 20:11–12, we are told that in that day the earth and the sky will flee and the dead will be gathered together before God's throne. Then the books will be opened and "The dead were judged according to what they had done as recorded in the books" (NIV). Those who worship the beast (Revelation 13:8) and accept the mark of the beast (Rev. 19:20), as well as the "cowardly, the unbelieving, the vile, the murderers, the sexually immoral, those who practice magic arts, the idolaters and all liars" (Rev. 21:8 NIV), will find themselves condemned. Then the second death will take place (Rev. 20:14, 21:8). Those whose names are written in the book of life will be spared (Rev. 20:15). God will dwell amongst them (Rev. 21:1–4) and "will wipe every tear from their eyes" (Rev. 21:4a NIV).

> "That day is a day of wrath,
> a day of trouble and distress,
> a day of destruction and desolation,
> a day of darkness and gloom,
> a day of clouds and total darkness…" (Zephaniah 1:15)

> "I will bring distress on mankind,
> and they will walk like the blind
> because they have sinned against the LORD.
> Their blood will be poured out like dust
> and their flesh like dung." (Zeph. 1:17)

> "Seek the LORD, all you humble of the earth,
> who carry out what he commands.
> Seek righteousness, seek humility;
> perhaps you will be concealed
> on the day of the LORD's anger." (Zeph. 2:3)

TIME OF REFLECTION

Go Deeper: Psalm 9

It is hard to be on the end that is being condemned. When we are in that place, we try to justify our behavior, dismiss it, ignore it, or find some other way to skip out on the judgment. Yet the only true way to have a chance of escaping judgment is to admit our complicity in the act for which we are being judged. While it may be painful in the moment, it is truly liberating in the long term. We admit our complicity, we change things to make them right, and then we ask for forgiveness. Where in our society does this need to happen? Where in your personal life do you need to take responsibility to make changes?

Now, after we have done this, how the person wronged responds is not in our control. They can reject our repentance and continue to condemn us, but then they become at risk of becoming the oppressor and continuing the cycle. Or they can accept our repentance and offer forgiveness to us in return, setting us both free. Where in our society do we need to start practicing forgiveness and stop the cycle of oppression? How does a lack of forgiveness keep the cycle of judgment going? Where in your personal life do you need to forgive?

In Jude 1:14–16, we read,

> "Enoch, the seventh from Adam, prophesied about these men: 'See, the Lord is coming with thousands upon thousands of his holy ones to judge everyone, and to convict all the ungodly of all the ungodly acts they have done in the ungodly way, and of all the harsh words ungodly sinners have spoken against him.' These men are grumblers and faultfinders; they follow their own evil desires; they boast about themselves and flatter others for their own advantage." (NIV)

Where is God inviting you to repent and seek God's mercy?

SON OF MAN – THE CHRIST

READ DANIEL 7:13–14, 27

These verses are like refreshing raindrops pouring upon a scorched dry land (Psalm 72:6). The significance of this moment is *huge!* The Messiah, who we now know as Jesus, is being introduced. Can you feel the excitement?

We see the passing of the baton between the Ancient of Days and the Son of Man. We once again read the repeated refrain, "His dominion is an everlasting dominion" (Daniel 2:44, 4:34, 6:26, 7:14, 27). There is this beautiful display of people from all nations and tongues serving him as the dominion, glory, and kingdom are given to this Messianic figure.

Remember as you read this that Daniel has not encountered the risen Messiah as the person Jesus. The first-century advent of Jesus as Messiah *(in Hebrew)* or Christ *(in Greek)* has not yet come. Daniel floats on a not-yet-fully-developed stream of Messianic expectation. So, we see a blending of this figure with the saints, both represented as "son of man," inheriting the kingdom (Dan. 7:22). Yet, at the end of verse 27, the kingdom is referred to as "His."

At the end of time, as we currently understand it, the loud voices of heaven and the seventh trumpet's blast will announce, "The kingdom of the world has become the kingdom of our Lord and of his Christ, and he will reign for ever and ever" (Revelation 11:15b NIV).

In contrast to the boisterous anti-Christ figure of the little horn, who destroys and does not deserve praise, we encounter this Hebraic "*bar enosh,*"[51] or one like a "son of man." This "Someone" or "ultimate human being,"[52] as otherwise translated, arrives on the scene and freely approaches the flaming-lit presence of the Ancient One. This is the first biblical reference to "son of man" as a yet-to-be-expected Messianic figure.[53]

In the New Testament, when Jesus identifies himself (Matthew 8:20, 9:6, 10:23, 12:40; Mark 14:41; Luke 6:5) and is identified by others as "the son of man," they are making reference back to this moment in Daniel.[54] The biblical theme of telling the history of kings is brought to culmination in the New

Testament with the arrival of Jesus in Israel, a man who arrives in Jerusalem on a colt and is welcomed by the waving of branches and the laying down of coats on the ground before him (Matt. 21:1–11, Mark 11:1–11, Luke 19:28–40, John 12:12–19). A man who is lifted up (John 19:16–30) and crowned with a crown of thorns (Matt. 27:29, Mark 15:17, John 19:2–5) and who we later see as the resurrected One ascending to heaven through the clouds (Acts 1:9–11). The man who, we are told, will return in the way that He departed, "coming on the clouds of heaven with power and great glory" (Matt. 24:30) to rule on this earth as its final and ultimate ruler.*

The day I moved into seminarian housing, Mr. Walter Peeler, the husband of a staff member, asked me, "When you are stuck between a rock and a hard place, which do you choose?" I had never heard this old saying rephrased as a question before, so I had to stop and think for a moment about how to answer. Then the light bulb went off in my mind, and I answered, "The rock." In Daniel 2:35, 44–45, we read of the establishment of the Messianic Kingdom being like a rock or a stone that strikes the idolatrous statue of past kingdoms and grows to become a great mountain. In Matthew 16:13–20, we hear that the great recognition that Jesus is the Messiah, the Son of the Living God, is the rock upon which the church will be built.

---

* It seems important to note, in a time period in which Artificial Intelligence is advancing such that computers can invent realistic-looking images of that which doesn't actually exist, that according to Revelation 1:7, when Jesus returns, every eye will witness his return. We are not to believe or go out to see just anyone who claims to be Jesus. No one will miss out on witnessing Jesus's return. See Matthew 24:23–31.

TIME OF REFLECTION

Go Deeper: Genesis 49:8–12, 24–25; Psalm 2

During the month of December, the season of Advent is celebrated by some Christians. This is the time leading up to Christmas Day and is considered the beginning of the church calendar. It serves as a reminder of how the Jewish people waited (and still wait) for the arrival of their Messiah. This season also points the Christian believer's attention to the fact that we are living in a time of Messianic expectation for Christ's second coming—we are in a second Advent season.

When we think of Christ's first advent and the combination of humility and glory that was expressed in the proclamation of Jesus's birth by the angels to the shepherds and then the humility of his birth among farm animals in contrast to his future return in glory with all people responding with fear and awe, not just the meek of Israel, we must recognize how little we know and how great is the One in whom we can place our hope. From a farmer's stall to clouds, from the glory of the cross to the glory of the worship of both heavenly hosts and human servants, to God be the praise!

Do you feel like you are living in a season of advent, awaiting the Messiah? How so?

How is today's reading an Easter Sunday reading?

"Look, he is coming with the clouds, and every eye will see him, even those who pierced him. And all the tribes of the earth will mourn over him. So it is to be. Amen" (Rev. 1:7). What is your response to this idea that every person will see Jesus and every tribe will recognize him when he returns?

How does seeing Jesus as the "rock" that can be chosen when stuck between a rock and a hard place reframe how you might handle difficult situations in the future?

KINGDOM OF SAINTS

READ DANIEL 7:18

S omeday, believers will govern. The separation of religious power from political power has been difficult to maintain. Something is inborn within humanity that wants to blur the two together. Perhaps it is our destiny. In verse 18, we first read about this future—the future in which "the saints of the Most High will receive the kingdom and will possess it forever."[55] This is the cry for the Holy City of Zion (Isaiah 60:14), a time in history and continuing beyond in which Jerusalem will be a place of prosperity and righteousness (Isa. 60–62).

And what should be our response to this future offer of the rule of God's Kingdom? We are to seek God's Kingdom (Luke 12:31), to worship God (Hebrews 12:28), and not to rely on material wealth now but to instead give generously to those in need (Luke 12:32–34).

We see the beginning of the fulfillment of this promise in the birth of Jesus, the descendant of David. Nathan the prophet speaks of an inheritor of God's promise to David, that David's offspring will "build a house for my Name, and I will establish the throne of his kingdom forever" (2 Samuel 7:13 NIV). The angel Gabriel who was sent to Mary proclaims, "The Lord God will give him the throne of his father David, and he will reign over the house of Jacob forever; his kingdom will never end" (Luke 1:32b–33 NIV). Later, as an adult, Jesus identifies himself in the Messianic words of Isaiah 61:1b "... the LORD has anointed me to preach good news to the poor ..." (NIV) (See also Luke 4:16–30.) We also see Jesus repeatedly speaking of the Kingdom of God. In fact, within the Gospels of Matthew through John, we read more uses of the word "kingdom" than the word "gospel."* A continuance of this movement toward the estab-

---

* The year prior to starting this devotional, I went through the books of Matthew, Mark, Luke, and John, and investigated what they proclaimed as the gospel. Much to my surprise, the emphasis was on the Kingdom of God. This is not to deny the importance of the good news of the gift of salvation received through the death and resurrection of Jesus Christ but to recognize that a primary emphasis of Jesus's teaching was the coming, and already here, Kingdom of God.

lishment of God's Kingdom on earth takes place at Pentecost with the establishment of the church (Acts 2). Even the writer of 1 Corinthians asks, "Do
you not know that the saints will judge the world?" (1 Corinthians 6:2a NIV).

In the last chapter of the book of Revelation, there is this beautiful imagery
of the tree of life planted on the banks of a crystal-clear river flowing from the
throne of God and of the Lamb. The curse on man from the days of Adam and
Eve is no longer, and the light of God radiates forth such that there is no need
for a sun. The prophet John writes that the servants of God will have God's
name written on their foreheads, and they will reign forever (Revelation 22:1–7).

Prior to this, in heaven a new song is sung,

"You [Jesus] are worthy to take the scroll
and to open its seals,
because you were slain,
and with your blood you purchased for God
persons from every tribe and language and people and nation.
You have made them to be a kingdom and priests to serve our God,
and they will reign on the earth." (Rev. 5:9–10 NIV)

Just as we have experienced the shift in history from BC ("before Christ")
to AD ("year of our Lord") with the incarnation of God's Son, Jesus, we will
experience another shift when He comes again. There is the time before the
ruling of the saints and the establishment of this last and eternal kingdom and
the time in which their reign takes place. Those who have shared in Christ's
sufferings will also share in his glory (Matthew 19:28–29, Romans 8:17) as
those who "endure … will also reign with him" (2 Timothy 2:12 NIV).

"'See, I will create
new heavens and a new earth.
The former things will not be remembered,
nor will they come to mind.
But be glad and rejoice forever
in what I will create,

for I will create Jerusalem to be a delight
and its people a joy.
I will rejoice over Jerusalem
and take delight in my people;
the sound of weeping and of crying
will be heard in it no more.

Never again will there be in it
an infant who lives but a few days,
or an old man who does not live out his years;
the one who dies at a hundred
will be thought a mere child;
the one who fails to reach a hundred
will be considered accursed.
They will build houses and dwell in them;
they will plant vineyards and eat their fruit.
No longer will they build houses and others live in them,
or plant and others eat.
For as the days of a tree,
so will be the days of my people;
my chosen ones will long enjoy
the work of their hands.
They will not labor in vain,
nor will they bear children doomed to misfortune;
for they will be a people blessed by the LORD,
they and their descendants with them.
Before they call I will answer;
while they are still speaking I will hear.
The wolf and the lamb will feed together,
and the lion will eat straw like the ox,
the dust will be the serpent's food.
They will neither harm nor destroy
on all my holy mountain,'
Says the LORD." (Isa. 65:17–25 NIV)

TIME OF REFLECTION

Go Deeper: Isaiah 60; Hebrews 12:22–29; 1 Peter 1:14–21

The idea of believers governing can be joyous for some, concerning for others, and still others may ask, "Which believers?" In Revelation 21:3 we read, "Now the dwelling of God is with men, and he will live with them. They will be his people, and God himself will be with them and be their God" (NIV). How does knowing that God will be present in a way that His love, righteousness, and truth will be unmistakable and intimate (and not lost to human interpretation) impact how you think of this final kingdom?

What do your political longings reveal about your desires for or against God's Kingdom? Do your longings align with Christ's mission on earth?

Psalm 145 to 146 describes the rule of God. In this we read,

> "He upholds the cause of the oppressed
>   and gives food to the hungry.
> The Lord sets prisoners free,
>   the Lord gives sight to the blind,
> the Lord lifts up those who are bowed down,
>   the Lord loves the righteous.
> The Lord watches over the foreigner
>   and sustains the fatherless and the widow,
>   but he frustrates the ways of the wicked."
> (Psalm 146:7-9 NIV)

What is the Kingdom of God like? According to Psalm 146:7–9, in what political and social actions should you take part?

OVERWHELMED

READ DANIEL 7:1, 9, 11, 13, 15–16, 28

I relate to Daniel's anguish and the turning of the complexion of his face due to receiving this vision. As I researched and read more about the little horn, I felt sick to my stomach. I could see some of the signs of the end times already evolving in my culture and place: people being deceived by a delusion and no longer being able to recognize the truth, rebellion within the Church, and apathy replacing love. If I let myself, I could identify the "man of lawlessness" described in 2 Thessalonians 2, often associated with "the arrogant little horn," with a contemporary person of influence. And yet, I remembered that in the past we have had other mini-anti-Christs, people like Heinrich Himmler, Sui Yang Di, Genghis Khan, Pol Pot, Nero, and Idi Amin. But to imagine any one of those men having an impact on a global scale sent me to the bathroom to empty my bowels.

And then we have the contrast of the magnificent imagery of the Ancient of Days and the coming of the Son of Man. This righteousness held in contrast to the previously revealed wickedness is overwhelming in a whole other way. The glory! The beauty! The relief of justice and the liberation! The making right of all that is so terribly wrong. And the Divine power trumping the frightening power of the human persecutor.

For some of us, this is the first time we've read such prophetic literature, and for others, we've heard the story so many times that the imagery no longer carries the drama for us. But no matter if this is your first reading or your fifth, consider what Daniel has just seen. No one has received imagery like this before him. He has not only seen a vision of destruction and glorification, but he has also seen a representative image of God! As is often expected, no one sees the image of God and lives. Yet, here Daniel lives to eventually tell the story and to prepare us for what is to come.

TIME OF REFLECTION

Go Deeper: Isaiah 24–26

When in your life have you been overwhelmed by a revelation of or about God?

How do you think you would have responded to receiving this vision in this manner?

What is your responsibility now that you have become aware of this vision?

ACTION

Take some time to seriously think about your current political values and the ways you speak about politics. Do the words you say and things you do represent a belief that God is our ultimate King and that you are supporting the values and work of the Kingdom of God as taught by Jesus?

How about other areas of your life? Do the ways you speak of other types of recognized figures, such as sports icons, celebrities, or even religious leaders, reflect Kingdom values? Do you give too much affection toward or allegiance to any one person or group? Does your community define your values, or does God define them?

How might God be calling you to recognize God's Kingdom established in Jesus Christ in the world today? What do you need to do to prepare to be a humble ruling saint in this Kingdom? Are you ready?

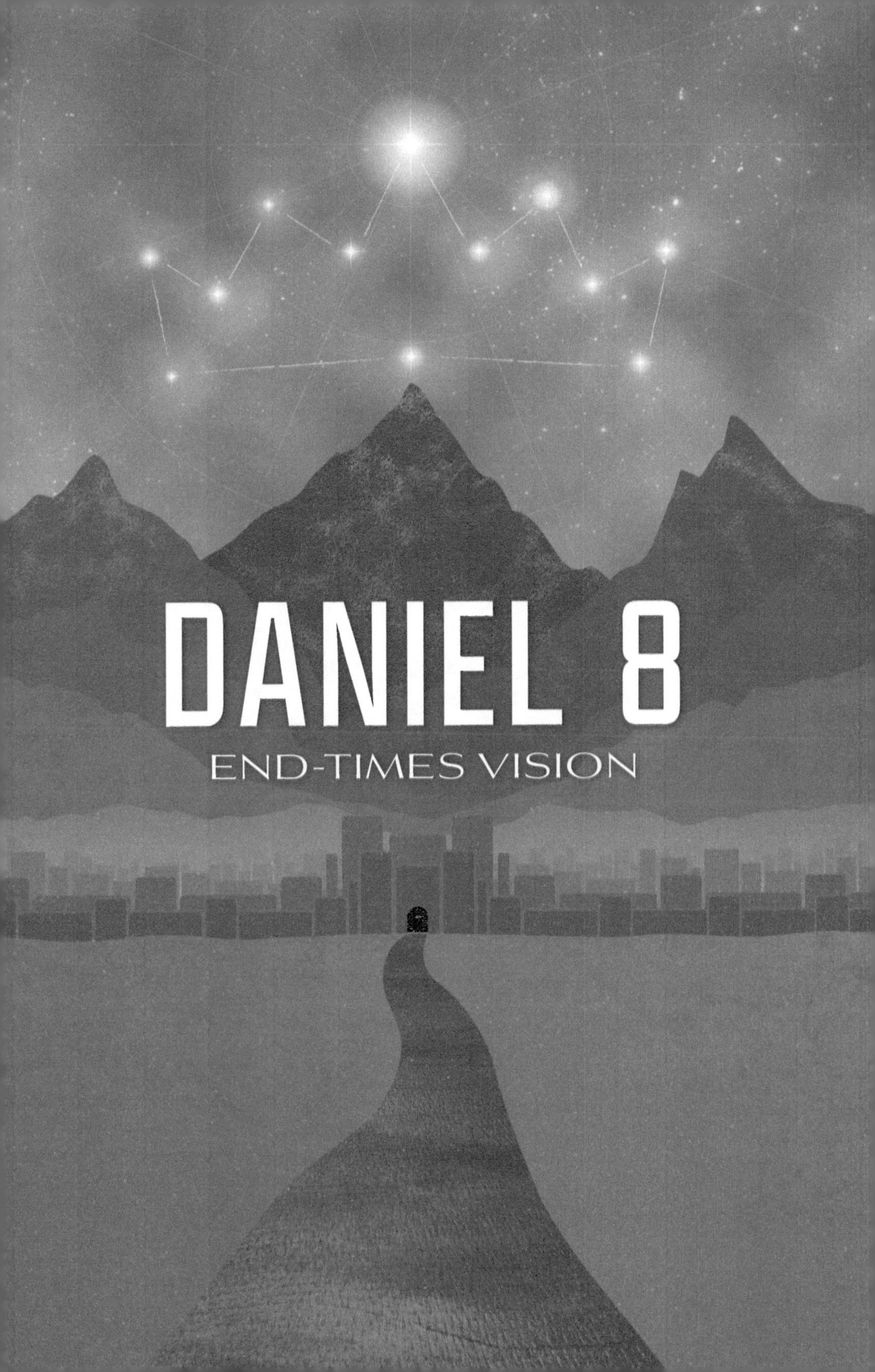
DANIEL 8
END-TIMES VISION

END-TIMES VISION

As we've seen so far, Daniel was a man gifted with understanding who could discern God's truth from God-given visions, dreams, and prayers. Yet, in chapter 8, he encounters a vision that stunts him. He requires assistance in understanding it, which is given to him by the appearance of the angel Gabriel. This is indeed an important message because Gabriel only appears to humans when there is a very important message to be shared. This is the angel who delivered the good news that Zechariah and Elizabeth, in their old age, would have their firstborn son John (Luke 1:19) and that Mary would be impregnated by the Holy Spirit and give birth to the Messiah (Luke 1:26–38). Yet in relaying this vision, Daniel, of all people, writes that he could not fully understand it.

At the time of this vision, Daniel is a provincial ruler governing in Babylon. He has a vision in which he is transported to the eastern edge of the empire to what is to become the capital of Persia, Susa (also known as Shushan; modern-day Shush in Khuzestan, Iran). This city east of the Tigris River and north of the Persian Gulf is to become a significant, prophetic location. It is here where the stories of Esther (Esther 1:2) and Nehemiah (Nehemiah 1:1) take place. This is where the Code of Hammurabi was later found inscribed in stone stele.[1] But Daniel doesn't know any of this. To him, this is the province of Elam, the son of Shem, the grandson of Noah (Genesis 10:1, 22, 31). Daniel's perception of the size of the world, although big for his time, is much smaller than what is being presented in this vision. This vision broadens his worldview, as kingdoms far greater than he likely has ever conceived are revealed to him. Daniel is considered far more educated than most, but unlike us, he has no three-dimensional globe to look at or World Wide Web to search. And yet, he finds himself by a canal known as the River Ulai, and it is here that he sees this vision, and then after seeking understanding hears a voice, likely God's, come from within these waters commanding Gabriel to explain.

Daniel responds with fear and trembling, falling to his face and into a deep sleep. Gabriel explains that this vision is about the "time of the end." Then Gabriel touches Daniel, waking him from his slumber, and continues to explain these "many days in the future"[2] that will take place at an appointed time and will be a time of "indignation"[3] or "wrath."[4] The end will come!

After receiving the vision, Daniel was overcome with depression and lay in bed sick for days. Then he got up, went back to work, and wrote down the words of this prophecy.

TIME OF REFLECTION

Go Deeper: 1 Peter 1:3–12; Revelation 22:10

In chapter 8, the language shifts from the commerce language of Gentiles, Aramaic, back to the language of Israel, Hebrew, which is also the language in which the book's introduction was written. If this were an intentional shift, what does it tell you about the intended audience for this vision and the ones, also written in Hebrew, that follow?

As a pastor, a common refrain I hear from people who are grieving are the words, "I don't know." When the vision came to a conclusion, there was still much of it that Daniel didn't understand. How might a lack of full understanding of the vision impact Daniel's experience of it? What emotions do you think he had? Grief? Despair?

Daniel was overcome with depression. The Bible does not ignore the reality of depression. In fact, this seems to be something with which prophets personally struggle. The great prophet Elijah, who had a personal and real relationship with God, came to a point in his ministry when he wanted God to end his life. God responded by allowing Elijah to rest, sending him food to eat, physically touching him through an angel, speaking softly to him, and restoring him with direction. You can read about this in 1 Kings 18–19.

As we see in the stories of Daniel, Elijah, Jeremiah, and Job, when we are depressed, God does not abandon us. Instead, God holds us in a loving embrace and tenderly cares for us. Have you ever been depressed? What helped you during that time of your life? Or, if you are currently feeling depressed, what help do you need now?

Many pastors, advocates, and passionate servant leaders get depressed from time to time. Understanding that depression does not indicate a lack of faith but at times may be the result of a great vision or faith, how does knowing this facilitate your care for these leaders?

THE RAM, THE GOAT, AND CONFRONTATION

READ DANIEL 8:3–8, 20–21

On the one hand, this section is full of precisely fulfilled prophecy that gives us assurance that God does what God says God will do (Joshua 21:45). On the other hand, this is prophecy that is yet to be fulfilled and a roadmap of what is to come. As we read about the ram and the goat and their confrontation, another layer of detail is added to previous visions.

If this vision took place in the third year of Belshazzar, as supported by the scroll fragments of the book of Daniel found at Qumran,[5] we are looking at a few years after 550 BC.[6] Cyrus II and his Persian empire have only been in existence for a little over a decade and have recently defeated the Medes, creating the Medo-Persian Empire.[7] This empire has barely begun, and yet, Daniel is given a vision in which Persia and Media are great powers in the Middle East. They are represented by the ram, which later in a first-century zodiac becomes associated with Persia[8] and its two horns, the first being the Medes and the longer coming up last as the Persians. Just as described, this empire pushed its way westward toward Israel and Babylon, northward toward Greece and Asia Minor, and southward toward Egypt in the west and India in the east. It is described as doing its own will and becoming great. We are told that no animal could withstand it, nor could anyone be delivered from its hand.

As Daniel stands beside the envisioned river, the curved-horn, woolly-coated male sheep is attacked by the thin-coated, pointed-horned male goat. Without touching the ground, this unicorned creature, representing the kingdom of Greece and its first very prominent king, travels in a savage rage "across the surface of the whole earth," attacking from the west. Scholars connect this goat with Greece and the notable horn with Alexander the Great, who, from 334 to 331 BC, beat Darius III of Persia.[9] In the time of Daniel, Greece was insignificant.

Yet, history tells us that Greece did conquer the Middle East from the west and that Alexander the Great was swift like the four-winged leopard of Daniel 7:6,[10] moving as though the ground was not there to resist him. To the people being conquered, it seemed as though he was conquering the whole earth.

The ram is powerless before the goat, and the goat breaks the ram's horns and tramples him to the ground. No one is able to help. As a result, the goat is strengthened, but as we have seen before in the book of Daniel, the proud are humbled, and the goat's large horn is broken. Or as we see with Alexander the Great, he dies suddenly at the age of thirty-three.[11]

We see this clear historical fulfillment, yet the interpretation that is given to Daniel is that these are the events that are to take place at the "time of the end." Remember how prophecy can be fulfilled multiple times, often near the time of the prophet delivering the message, again during the time of Jesus, and yet again at the end. When we read chapter 8, we need to pay attention to the parts that stand out as not yet making sense, as these may still have a future fulfillment. For example, this idea that the goat will arrive by crossing the surface of the whole earth without touching the ground does not appear to be literally fulfilled in ancient times, nor during the first coming of the Christ. Yet, reading it in contemporary times, it sounds like air travel. This then makes us also wonder if other elements of the vision could have alternative meanings in the future. Perhaps "Media" is actually "media," considering that the "horn" could refer to social media, as one of the oldest social media platforms was formed by a person with that last name.[12] Or maybe these symbols are acronyms, like New York's Geographic Online Address Translator (G.O.A.T.)[13]* But to be less fantastical and a little less conspiratorial, these countries still exist. Persia is now present-day Iran, and Greece is a country in southeast Europe. Pretty amazing that they are still here after all these years!

---

* Both of these imaginative interpretations are from a Western, English-speaking perspective. They are not intended to be taken seriously but rather are there to encourage the reader to recognize that the meaning of this passage could still be mysterious.

TIME OF REFLECTION

Go Deeper: Deuteronomy 18:15–22; 1 Peter 1:10–12

Scholars are fascinated by the specificity in which this prophecy was fulfilled by Persia and Greece. As a result, some have concluded that there is no way this could have been written prior to the life of Alexander the Great. Yet, the Bible is full of prophecy, and the Bible uses the fulfillment of prophecy as an argument for the credibility of God's Word. Those who accept that Daniel recorded this prophecy during his lifetime explain that the detail of fulfillment gives the reader confidence that the parts of prophecy that have not yet been fulfilled will be in the future.

How does your view on the dating of the writing of Daniel impact your view on prophecy, or how does your view on prophecy impact how you date the writing of Daniel?

Which comes first for you: Your beliefs about prophecy or your beliefs about the dating of Daniel? Why?

What would happen if you took the opposite view? How would that impact your faith?

If you were to view the story of the ram and goat as an unfulfilled prophecy, what traits would you look for in a political leader or a country that would fulfill this vision?

HORNS AGAIN

——————————— READ DANIEL 8:8–11, 22–25 ———————————

Arising from the goat's broken horn comes four horns representing four less powerful kingdoms—the four winds of heaven. Again, many scholars see this as the death of Alexander the Great and the division of his empire into four parts.[14,15] If interpreting in this manner, the four kingdoms are: (1) Macedonia and Greece, (2) Thrace and Asia Minor, (3) northern Syria, Mesopotamia, and Babylon, (4) southern Syria, Palestine, and Egypt.[16,17] We read that near the end of the four kingdoms' rule, transgression and rebellion will reach capacity.

Then, from one of four kingdoms comes a little horn, a new king—which, like in Daniel 7, grows to be great. Again, we see this new and emerging horn associated by commentators with Antiochus IV Epiphanes, who came out of one of the previous four horns: the Seleucid kingdom.[18] Remember, this is the man who killed and enslaved the people of Israel, replaced their worship of God with the worship of an idol, and forbade Jewish religious practice. He even went so far as to sacrifice a pig on the Temple altar, which was considered a sinister desecration.[19]

His kingdom grows to be great in three directions: toward the south, east, and the "Glorious Land," which is Israel. And then it grows toward the "host of heaven"—this brings our attention to the otherworldly nature or spiritual impact of this kingdom. Its reach expands beyond the earth to the divine realm. For the Babylonians, this would be the assembly of the gods; for the Hebrews, it might refer to God's angelic council, or generally draws our attention to outer space;[20] and for modern Christians, this may refer to the Church or the spiritual realm.

Once again, we read of the character of this anti-Christ figure as one who spreads deception, is intentionally sinister, is destructive toward the powerful and the holy, and gains great power. And remarkably, he goes against the army of heaven itself!

TIME OF REFLECTION

Go Deeper: Genesis 3

As I write this devotional, many in my culture would say that "truth has been thrown to the ground" (Daniel 8:12). Not everyone would agree with *how* this prospering of deceit began, but most would say it is happening. In Daniel 8, the little horn is given responsibility for causing "deceit to prosper" due to his "cunning" and "influence." How can one person influence culture so dramatically?

How have you seen a person have influence like this during your lifetime?

What, if anything, can a person or a group of people do to counteract a deceitful power?

In Genesis 3:15, we read about the punishment that came as a result of Adam and Eve disobeying God—the first sin committed on this new earth. The serpent who deceived the woman is told by God that "I will put hostility between you and the woman, and between your offspring and her offspring. He will strike your head, and you will strike his heel." Since the birth of Jesus, some have come to see this use of "He" as a representation of Jesus crushing the head of Satan. How do you see a cosmic conflict presented in the text of Daniel 8?

Read Genesis 3. How does the re-creation story of end times counter the fall of creation story in Genesis? What role do deception and truth play in each story? Is truth or deception ultimately victorious?

THE REBELLION

For many years, I drove past a banner hung from a downtown Catholic Church that read, "Join us for perpetual adoration." Being a Protestant Christian, I didn't understand what was being advertised, but it caught my attention and my curiosity. So one day, I decided to pull over and go inside and ask. Luckily, the first person I met was the youth pastor, a person experienced in explaining religious practices in accessible ways. He pointed out a small room in which people were kneeling in prayer. Inside this room, those present recognized the presence of Christ in the wafer used in the Eucharist known as the "Host." The Host was in a prominent position in what I would identify as the altar of this small chapel. This congregation had committed to a twenty-four-hour, seven-days-a-week adoration of Christ. I asked if I could enter the room and was given permission to do so.

Although this was all new to me, and I come from a tradition in which the elements of communion are symbolic and we recognize Christ's presence in the presence of the believers gathered to take part together rather than in the bread, I entered with respect and lifted my attention in prayer toward God. I was surprised to be overwhelmed by a sense of God's presence, and unexpectedly, tears began to trickle down my cheek.

When I first read the words "exalted himself as high as the Prince of the host,"[21] the image and idea of Jesus receiving twenty-four-seven attention in a downtown church in my community come to mind. For Daniel, the image likely would have been of the Temple in Jerusalem and the sacrifices made by the priests on behalf of the people as they looked to our holy God for mercy. I am reminded that God is worthy of our full attention and that in heaven, worship is perpetual. If we look at humanity as a whole, or even this church in my city, worship of God on earth is also meant to be perpetual. So, what arrogance it would take for one to "exalt himself in his heart" to "rise against" God and God's representatives.

When we read of the removal of daily sacrifices, we understand that for Daniel, it meant a future date after the Temple would be rebuilt. This hadn't yet happened, and so while being a message of despair, it would also be a message of hope that his people would indeed return to the Promised Land and again offer sacrifices. If it wasn't a future date, then it referred to Daniel's present moment and the great sadness he and his people felt being in captivity, knowing that the morning and evening sacrifices of the lamb (Numbers 28:1–8) were not being offered at home.

TIME OF REFLECTION

Go Deeper: John 14:1–17

Antiochus Epiphanes stopped Jewish sacrifices in the rebuilt Temple in 167 BC and made a pagan sacrifice there on the fifteenth of Kislev that year.[22] Even in choosing the name "Epiphanes," which translates as "glorious one," we see Antiochus fulfilling this scripture by claiming to be God.[23] How do you see the worship of God being trampled in religious institutions today?

Who do you see, if anyone, exalting themselves in their heart to the place of God?

2,300 DAYS

The message of Daniel has been unsealed. The book is sitting in front of us as part of the Christian canon. It is readily available for reading throughout the world, although some of its meaning may remain veiled. It is in this context that we read of two holy ones explaining the time period from start to finish in which the regular sacrifice is not offered, the rebellion takes place, and the sanctuary and holy army are trampled. But the good news is that at the end of this time, the sanctuary will be cleansed!

This is what Hanukkah celebrates—the eight-day cleansing of the Temple after Antiochus Epiphanes desecrated it. This is what Easter celebrates—the replacement of the morning and evening sacrifice of a lamb (Numbers 28:1–8) with the once-and-for-all sacrifice of the Holy Lamb of God, Jesus (Hebrews 10:1–25). This was indeed a key turning point in which a time of wrath was replaced by a time of mercy, in which we now live. This was a symbolic reminder to Daniel that his people would one day once again worship God in the Temple. And this is what we will celebrate again at the time of the end.

The length of time in question here is very specific. The numbering must be important because it is with this number that the holy ones begin their explanation of the vision.

How do we understand this number? A day is described in the text as having an evening and morning. So, it would be appropriate to understand the number as representing the total number of twenty-four-hour time periods that will occur between the desecration of the Temple and its rededication. This would equal a little over six years. Yet, some have faithfully argued that mornings and evenings are being counted separately, totaling 2,300 sacrifices, so there are instead 1,150 days (three years and two months) between these events. Others have argued that a "day" in prophetic literature could be understood as a place marker for a year, as in 2,300 years.

There have been various attempts to interpret this number literally, historically, and approximately. For example, 1,150 days could align with the three-year (360-day year) plus ancient Greek leap months (60 days) and an additional 10-day time period[24] between the desecration (fifteenth of Kislev, 167 BC) and the reconsecration (twenty-fifth of Kislev, 164 BC) of the Temple during the time of the Maccabees.[25] Another example could be 2,300 days between the beginning of the animosity between Antiochus and the Jews (171 BC) and the later cleansing of the Temple from its defilement (165 BC).[26] If you search the internet, you can find people starting the count with the rise of Antiochus and continuing 2,300 years forward to the present day. Personally, I wonder what role the destruction of the Second Temple by Titus in 70 AD could have had in the discussion. I also wonder if the start date of the 2,300 mornings and evenings has begun more recently (Av 5779/August 2019,* Passover 5780/March 2020†) or if the start date still remains to be fulfilled. What do you think?

---

* On August 30, 2019 (29 Av 5779), I had this sense that the beginning of the end had begun. Interestingly, unbeknownst to me at the time, both the destruction of the First Temple and the Second Temple took place during the month of Av.

† Passover 5780 was the first time much of the globe went into their homes, closed their doors, and waited for the angel of death to pass over. This was due to the COVID-19 pandemic. The world knowingly and unknowingly practiced a Passover ritual. Meanwhile, a group of priests assembled at the Temple Mount, ready to make the Passover sacrifice, which had not been offered there since the destruction of the Second Temple in 70 AD.

TIME OF REFLECTION

Go Deeper: John 2:13–25

We can interpret the eighth chapter of Daniel in several ways. We could understand the events in this chapter as already fulfilled or yet to be fulfilled. Some would argue that these events marked the path toward the first coming of Christ, while others might say they show what will happen prior to Christ's second coming. How do you interpret the events of chapter 8? Why do you choose that interpretation?

Why do you think the angels would reveal a specific number regarding the fulfillment of this passage?

If you were to "invent" a prophecy, would you include specific details or would you keep it more generalized? Why?

What makes this prophecy believable or unbelievable?

ACTION

At some point, we may consider the possibility that the prophecies of Daniel are pointing to a date that is still in the future. If this is the case, these prophesies give us hints as to what to be watching for to know that the end is near. Take time to reflect upon what you have already read in Daniel and what you have learned. Create a timeline of end-times events based on a presupposition that what Daniel foretells is yet to occur. Or make a time-line of events, seeing them as already fulfilled.

You are welcome to use the following from Daniel 8 as a starting point:

1. The kings of Media and Persia, with the Persian king coming up last, will push westward, northward, and southward and become great.

2. Then, without touching the ground, in a rage, the first king of Greece will travel across the surface of the earth, coming from the west, to confront the kings of Media and Persia.

3. Media and Persia will be powerless before this king and will be trampled to the ground.

4. Although the first king of Greece becomes powerful and great, he eventually is broken, and four less powerful kings from Greece take his place.

5. Near the end of their kingdoms, when rebellion has reached its full capacity, from one of the four kingdoms will emerge a ruthless, deceptive, and prosperous king. His kingdom will grow toward the south, east, the "Glorious Land" (Israel), and the hosts of heaven.

6. This king will destroy the mighty and holy ones. He will cast down the sanctuary, remove the daily sacrifices, and make deceit prosper.

7. After 2,300 evenings and mornings, the time of the rebellion will come to an end and the sanctuary will be cleansed.

DANIEL 5

(And so we return to Chapter 5.)

WRITING ON THE WALL

TEMPLE VESSELS

─────────── READ DANIEL 5:1–4, 22–24 ───────────

In October 539 BC,[1] the interim and acting king, Belshazzar, holds a grand banquet for his thousands of nobles and innumerable wives and concubines. While foreign invaders plan a stealthy invasion of Babylon's stronghold, Belshazzar undermines his governing responsibilities by wasting himself on alcohol and other indulgences, all in front of his subjects. In a state of unregulated arrogance, Belshazzar calls for the sacred vessels of the Jews: gold and silver cups that had been consecrated for Divine purposes. Vessels whose sacred holiness could not be removed by their removal from the Temple or their improper use by a foreign king. That which is holy remains holy to God!

Whether he meant to mock the God who gives us life, to injure his Jewish subjects, to seek the protection of the Babylonian gods against an approaching enemy, or was just being foolish, he had the crowd raise a glass to the lifeless gods of wood, stone, and metal. Did the heavens thunder as this took place? Did the angels observe with pain in their eyes? It obviously got God's attention. As we will see in later verses, God sends the holy prophet Daniel to deliver with boldness the message of God's already prepared response: You have not glorified "the God who holds your breath in His hand and owns all your ways..."[2]

TIME OF REFLECTION

Go Deeper: Matthew 21:12–13; Hebrews 10

Do we have objects today that have been consecrated for God? If so, how does today's Scripture reading instruct us about how we are to treat those objects?

The word "sacrilege" is used to describe the misuse of that which is regarded as sacred. Blasphemy is profane talk against that which is holy. Desecration takes place when violence is dealt toward that which is sacred. How do you know if something is a sacrilegious offense, blasphemous word, or a desecrating act? Where have you seen or heard disrespect of a sacred person, place, or thing?

If a person were to set a can of soda pop on a church communion table, would this be considered sacrilegious? Why or why not?

GOD GETS THE
RULER'S ATTENTION!

READ DANIEL 5:5–9

W hat is it like to see the finger of God engraving your fate on a wall? For Belshazzar, it elicited fear. Or as the English version of the Hebrew goes, "It scared the crap out of him," or as politely translated, "He soiled himself and his knees knocked together."[3] Belshazzar was frightened by the thoughts that entered his mind. He didn't know what the words said, but he had a sense of divine judgment, and this drew to his mind all the possibilities that such judgment could bring. Whether this was guilt related to certain incidences, including the use of the Jewish sacred vessels while calling upon false gods, or thoughts about the Persian army that was actively conquering city by city and heading his way,[4] we don't know. But we do know it was enough to cause him to ask for help from the wise men of the land. God had gotten his attention!

Imagine the setting in which this all took place: The extravagant party was likely gathered in the 170-by-55-foot throne room.[5] According to archeological finds, this room was built with blue glazed brick walls, which were accented with deep red designs. Mosaics of lions bordered the base of these walls. Looking out through the room's grand entry, the courtyard could be seen. I imagine the lampstand is lit and the flickering light reflects off the plastered wall where the armless fingers of a hand appear.

What did this hand look like? It was not embodied, was it? Was it severed? Did the wrist fade into the cloak of darkness? What was its size? Was it like that of a human or that of a god? We know that even though it appeared as human fingers, its source is recognized as God. Exodus makes reference to the "finger of God" inscribing the law on the stone tablets (Exodus 31:18), and the Egyptian magicians referred to the plague of gnats as "the finger of God" (Ex. 8:19).

Belshazzar recognizes the significance of the message even if he doesn't know the message's exact meaning. So he offers an incentive—the person who can explain what he and others just witnessed will be lifted up to the position just below his.* Yet, no one steps forward to claim the award.

TIME OF REFLECTION

Go Deeper: Psalm 103:11–13; John 8:1–11

My mother tells me that when I was very young, I wrote on the wall with a crayon one night when I was supposed to be sleeping. The next morning, I told her that I didn't know who did it; it must have been a mouse. Sometime later, we were in a store and I found a stuffed toy mouse I wanted. When I asked my mom if she'd buy the mouse for me, she responded, "I don't know if we can have any more mice in the house because they write on the walls while we are asleep." I quickly confessed my wrongdoing, said I would never do it again, and I went home with a stuffed toy mouse. I learned from that experience that my mom wasn't as disappointed about the crayon on the wall as she was about me lying to her about it.

We all have lied or done something wrong at some point in our lives. One gift we have as humans is the gift of true guilt that leads us to right our wrongs. One of the interesting qualities of guilt that comes from God is that we usually know the exact reason for feeling guilty, even if we aren't willing to admit it.

There are other forms of guilt that are not from God, and these usually don't offer us any room for repentance or for making things right. There is the false guilt that comes from being manipulated. Or the guilt that comes from breaking cultural rules that have no moral, ethical, or true relational consequence. Sometimes an emotion such as grief or a struggle such as perfectionism is mislabeled as "guilt."

Sometimes our response to true guilt that we need to deal with is a dismissive joy and thrill-seeking, kind of like what we see in Belshazzar in this story.

---

* There is a general understanding among historical commentators that Belshazzar is standing in for his father and that he doesn't have full power as king. This would mean that he is second in power, and whoever interpreted the writing on the wall would be ranked next as third.

Is there anywhere in your life where you are experiencing guilt that is from God? What are you going to do about it?

Is there anywhere in your life where you are experiencing false guilt or another emotion or struggle mislabeled as guilt? Are you willing to let go of this and entrust this to God?

KING BELSHAZZAR VERSUS BELTESHAZZAR (DANIEL)

──────── READ DANIEL 5:10–17, 22–23 ────────

O ur given names carry meaning. I shared a good chuckle with the first child I baptized when together we discovered the meaning of his first name, "crooked nose" or "crooked river." On the other hand, the first baby I dedicated during a worship service was named "Glory" after God's Shekinah Glory. In the Bible, we see the intentional selection of names often chosen to honor God, bring memory to an occasion, represent character, or symbolically foreshadow a future judgment. When Abraham and Sarah heard on separate occasions that after decades of infertility, they would become parents together, they each laughed, and thus their first child was named "Isaac," which means "to laugh" (Genesis 17:17, 18:9–15, 21:1–8). The prophet Isaiah and an unnamed prophetess named one of their children "Maher-shalal-hash-baz," meaning "Swift is the booty, speedy is the prey," to confirm the events that were about to take place (Isaiah 8:1–4).

Our main character Daniel carries a name that honors "El," the God worshipped by the Hebrews. His name means "God is my judge." His friends have similar God-honoring names: Hananiah or "The LORD shows grace," Mishael or "Who is what God is?" and Azariah, meaning, "The LORD helps."[6] But when Daniel received his Babylonian name, "-el" was replaced with "Bel-" lifting up the Babylonian god, Bel. Daniel's Babylonian name, "Belteshazzar," could be understood as "Bel, protect his life!"[7] or "Bel, protect the king,"[8] even though Daniel knew it was truly the God "El" who would protect him.

Did you notice the similarity between names in this chapter? It is as if a contrast is being drawn between these two men who basically bear the same name. Someone has suggested that the younger was named after the elder. But if the parent had desired for the recipient of the name to model the traits of Belteshazzar, it would have been more appropriate to name him "Daniel," lifting up the name of the God of the Hebrews who informed Daniel's character and blessed him with insight, intelligence, and wisdom. Yet, Belteshazzar seems unknown to Belshazzar. In his humility and faith, Belteshazzar doesn't seem to have a need to prove himself or to accept the honor offered by Belshazzar. He is content in his own identity and relationship with God and does not need to be validated by the new and passing arrogant human ruler.

TIME OF REFLECTION

Go Deeper: Genesis 2:18–25

What does your name mean?

Did those who named you know the meaning of your name when they gave it to you? Why did they choose this name for you?

Do you think your name is representative of your character? Why or why not?

THE INSCRIPTION'S MEANING

READ DANIEL 5:13–16, 25–31

G od had prepared Daniel for this moment. His and Nebuchadnezzar's previous visions gave Daniel the clear expectation that Babylon would come to an end and the Medes and Persians would take over. He may have even been aware of the prophet Jeremiah's prophecy about the Medes conquering Babylon and that Babylon's leaders, wise men, and warriors would be drunk, not waking again from their sleep (Jeremiah 51:11, 57). Parts of the Babylonian empire had already fallen prior to the events of this story, and from Daniel's observations of the condition of the thousands gathered at this party, he likely could see the vulnerability of this unconquerable city at this very moment. If there were a time for the enemy to strike, it would be now.

All the king's drunken wise men could not interpret the message. The queen, likely the queen mother or sister, upon hearing the fear-filled noisy commotion coming from the banquet hall and the loud cry for the idolatrous diviners to intervene, intervened herself by saying to consult Daniel.

The words that appeared on the wall would have been familiar in the Babylonian tongue while likely written in the Aramaic script of the Hebrew people, such that the vowels and possibly even spaces between words were absent, making it unreadable to some.[9] In English, they would have appeared as "Numbered, Numbered, Weigh, Divide." Or something along the idea of "Quarter, Quarter, Nickel, Dime," as Babylonian monetary units listed in order from the greatest weight down to the least weight,[10] with the duplication of the first word emphasizing that the time is now. The message may have only been readable by someone like Daniel, who was of the chosen people and familiar with adding the vowels to the Hebrew script as well as attuning to God's voice. Thus it appears that God spoke in such a way that required Daniel to be there to interpret. So Daniel announces the condemnation: Belshazzar and his kingdom were weighed on a balance and found wanting. The time had come for their end and for the kingdom to be given to two nations. The very night they sacrilegiously, in a drunken stupor, offer praise to idols using the sacred vessels of the one true God is the night they are conquered.

TIME OF REFLECTION

Go Deeper: Jeremiah 51

How has God been preparing Daniel for this very moment?

Have you had any experience in your life where you felt as though several prior experiences prepared you for that exact moment? If not in your life, have you seen this occur in someone else's life, where they were the right person at the right time with the right preparation to do the right thing? If not someone you know, someone perhaps that you've read about or learned about through others?

Do you see a theme in your life that may not yet be fulfilled? What is that theme? How are you listening or waiting on God for its fulfillment?

VALUE OF INTER-GENERATIONAL DIALOGUE

READ DANIEL 5:17–24

One challenge of a new job is figuring out how to relate to one's predecessor. This can be especially challenging in a position of leadership or management in which you have the power to make independent decisions. A predecessor understands the culture of a workplace, and as her tenure comes to its fullness, her decision-making is often impacted by institutional knowledge of what the outcome of the decision may be. Whereas someone new to a position offers the gift of a fresh perspective that isn't encumbered by institutional knowledge. This creates new flexibility and growth for an organization but also carries the risk of dismantling important systems that protect the organization and its members from harm. The lack of historical institutional knowledge can negatively impact the foresight of the immature leader. A healthy transition usually includes a recognition of the past, a willingness to learn from it, and a commitment to take advantage of the moment to bring about much-needed change that may be informed by that understanding of the past and shaped by a vision for the future.

We can see this in the intergenerational exchange as well. The young bring in a fresh, new perspective, ready to get rid of old patterns that have caused harm, while the old remind the young of why those patterns exist, pointing out their value and challenging them to find the nuance so the generations together can create something even better—the best from both perspectives. Unfortunately, this doesn't happen often, as we aren't willing to take the time to listen and to understand, and so we repeat the cycles we are trying to break.

In Daniel 5, we read, "your predecessor ... your predecessor ..." (verse 11), "your predecessor ..." (verse 18), and then we come to this most revealing of statements, "But you his successor, Belshazzar, have not humbled your heart, even though you knew all this." Had he only been humble enough to listen to the stories from those who came before him, Belshazzar might have been wise enough to recognize that "The Most High God is ruler over human kingdoms and sets anyone he wants over them."[11] He might have considered Daniel as an advisor rather than needing the queen to remind him of Daniel's insight, intelligence, and wisdom. He might have realized that if he acted boisterously, offending the God of the Hebrews (the one true God as God came to be understood by his predecessor), then he would be at risk of being humbled, similar to what had taken place for Neb. For the original reader of this text, "predecessor" would have included an acknowledgment of all who came before Belshazzar as those whose shoes he now walked in. Belshazzar was the last to walk in those shoes.

TIME OF REFLECTION

Go Deeper: Acts 7

One area where many changes have occurred at the turn of this last century and where intergenerational dialogue about the changes seems to be missing is in conversations about what defines "family" and how "family" is or isn't understood to be an essential societal institution. These conversations seem to take place most frequently within a generation but not across generations. This can easily be seen by reading news articles on this topic from each decade over the last hundred years. There is a clear discrepancy between each generation's dialogue. How might more intentional listening and understanding across generations be helpful?

How have you seen a workplace employee or management transition go well? What contributed to a successful transition between people?

Who are your ancestors, and what have you learned from them? Can you think of a time when you wished you would have listened better to your ancestors?

In this story, we see a contrast between Neb's response to God and Belshaz-zar's unconverted death. What can we learn from the contrast between these two leaders?

ACTION

─────── RE-READ DANIEL 5 ───────

What are some ways that you have dethroned God and put yourself in God's place? Sit with this question today and invite God's Spirit to show you the way.

DANIEL 9

(And so we skip ahead to Chapter 9.)

TIME OF COMPLETION

DARIUS AND CYRUS

———————— READ DANIEL 6:1, 6, 28; 9:1–2; 10:1; 10:20–11:1 ————————

An interesting situation takes place as we look at the remaining chapters. The timeline becomes a bit confusing as reference is made to two kings: Darius of the Medes and Cyrus of Persia. As we slow down and examine the text closely, we discover the following:

- Chapter 5 – ends with Darius the Mede taking over Belshazzar's kingdom.

- Chapter 6 – begins with Darius and ends with a mention of both Darius and Cyrus. This chapter could be considered a summary or setup chapter of all that is to follow in the last quarter of the book. It concludes the first half of Daniel, but its historical timing is unclear. We don't know if it takes place prior to, at the same time as, or after the prayer recorded in chapter 9. Keep this in mind as you read chapter 6 and reflect back on the prayer of chapter 9.

- Chapter 9 – takes place during the first year of Darius.

- Chapter 10 – takes place during the third year of Cyrus.

- Chapter 11 – takes place during the third year of Cyrus but makes reference back to the first year of Darius, implying that the first year of his reign is in the past.

One of these kings, Cyrus the Great, has been recognized by history; the second, Darius, has had both his existence and identity questioned. Who is Darius the Mede? Is he a co-regent with Cyrus? Is he ruling over the Medes and Chaldeans,* while Cyrus rules over the Persians? Is this a ruler who comes

———————————————————————————————————————
* The Chaldeans are the indigenous people who were conquered by the Babylonians and then later ruled by the Medes and Persians.

after Cyrus, or is this another name for Cyrus?[1] Or if we want to interpret symbolically, could we say the message here is a cryptic code that will unveil a greater revelation at a future time?

The ancient commentator Jerome argued that Cyrus and Darius together overcame Babylon, yet there remained a distinctiveness between their two kingdoms, and Darius, being the elder relative, took reign over Babylon and took Daniel home to be within his court of the Medes.[2] Theodoret of Cyr, also writing in the 400s AD, joins Jerome in recognizing two different rulers named Darius, one who was a Mede living during the time of Belshazzar, and a second Darius, the Persian[3] who lived much later. [4] The modern *Global Study Bible* places Darius after Cyrus, with Cyrus issuing a decree ending the exile in 538 BC and sixteen years later, in 522 BC, Darius taking the throne.[5] In our devotional reading, we will take the book of Daniel at face value, assuming that Darius is a real king who was a contemporary of King Cyrus II (the Great).

TIME OF REFLECTION

Go Deeper: Proverbs 21:1; 1 Timothy 2:1–4; Colossians 1:16

How have the actions of the kings mentioned in Daniel helped move the story forward throughout the book?

What role do these kings have in the story of the Hebrew people?

Why are they important in telling the story of how God relates to humanity?

Daniel is a man with the integrity of faith, and he governs under rulers who don't share that same faith. What can we learn from Daniel about how we are to live in the world today?

SEVENTY

—————————— READ DANIEL 9:1–2, 11–14 ——————————

S o much of the Bible is a setup for the next part of the Bible. This is part of what gives it credibility. While it is commonly understood that about forty authors wrote the Bible over 1,500 years, it is incredible how the different parts link together. Take the significance of the number "seventy" in this chapter as an example.

We'll start in Genesis. The first great funeral memorial was held in Egypt for seventy days over the death of Jacob, also known as Israel (Genesis 50:1–14). The Hebrew people were living in Egypt, a place later remembered for captivity. At the end of their mourning, they traveled to Canaan to bury their patriarch there, thus returning him to the Promised Land a symbolic seventy days later.

Moving on to Exodus, we read of seventy elders of Israel being invited into God's presence to witness God with their very own eyes! God and Israel make a legal covenant. As part of this covenant, the seventy elders and the people commit to "do and obey all that the LORD has commanded" (Exodus 24:1–11). When they later renew this covenant, it is explicitly stated that if they don't honor their end of the agreement, they will be taken into captivity and dispersed among foreign lands until they repent and return to God in faithfulness and obedience. Only then will the land be opened back up to them (Deuteronomy 27–30). Seventy elders act as witnesses to the covenant—later, seventy years act as a witness to the breaking of the covenant. And in Daniel 9, for the first and only time in this book, God is referred to as Yahweh and is identified with this covenantal-referencing name seven times![6]

We also read in the book of Numbers that the Spirit of God came to rest upon seventy elders so they could assist Moses in governing the people (Numbers 11:16–30). Far into the future, Jesus anoints seventy disciples to assist Him in His work of ministry (Luke 10).

We even see the significance of faithfulness and faithlessness associated with the number seventy when we read about worship spaces. When setting up the tabernacle, a leader from each of the twelve tribes faithfully donated a seventy-shekel silver bowl full of fine flour mixed with oil for a grain offering (Num. 7). But much later, when Ezekiel was given a vision of the detestable, faithless acts of Israel in which they broke the covenant that paved the way for their captivity, he saw seventy elders offering incense to idols in the Temple of God (Ezekiel 8)! Even King Solomon was told that someday Israel would be cut off due to their worship of false gods (1 Kings 9:1–9).

In the collection of Psalms, we read that seventy years is the average life span of a person (Psalm 90:10) and Isaiah calls seventy years "the life span of one king" (Isaiah 23:15). In the Pentateuch, we read that the Hebrew people were punished with wandering in the wilderness until the passing of the generation that was unwilling to trust God for the strength to enter Canaan (Num. 32:13). So, it would be within the pattern that the Babylonian captivity would also last a life span.

As the seventieth year of their exile approaches, God begins to speak to his prophets that it is time to rally the people. Studious Daniel, who has access to written prophecies, discovers that Jeremiah had prophesied that Nebuchadnezzar would conquer them and they would serve Babylon for seventy years (Jeremiah 25:9–11), and then the people would return to God and God would return them to their land (Jer. 29:10–14). Not long after this, Zechariah hears the Lord speak, "The LORD was extremely angry with your ancestors … This is what the LORD of Armies says: Return to me … and I will return to you …" (Zechariah 1:2–3). Later in Daniel chapter 9, we will read of the announcement that the seventy weeks will end, reconcile, bring in, seal up, and anoint.

Prior to this point, Daniel seemed to accept his people's fate of dispersion and captivity amongst foreign lands, but Jeremiah's prophecy seems to wake him up to the possibility that this, too, will come to an end. It is time for his people to repent and return!

Reading Jeremiah's prophecy may also reframe for us Neb's dream of the tree. Seven periods of time were declared for the humbling of the human being. Perhaps this vision wasn't just for Neb but also a reminder to Israel that, like the tree, they had been cut down with only a stump and roots left, waiting for regrowth. They had been bound in iron and bronze but would one day be restored (Daniel 4:23, 26). Perhaps there is even a message here for the Church of a future time as well.

TIME OF REFLECTION

Go Deeper: Jeremiah 25:11–12, 29:10–15

Daniel continually sought wisdom from God, and God continually responded by giving Daniel understanding. James 1:5–6 instructs us to ask with faith for wisdom from God. How have you sought God's wisdom since beginning this study on the book of Daniel?

Is the number seventy significant to you in any way?

How do you see the generations before you being blessed or cursed because of the choices they made during their lives?

How will the generations that follow yours be impacted by both the faithful and faithless decisions that your generation has made?

Are you currently living in a seventy-year epoch of either faithfulness or faithlessness?

THE PRAYER

—————————— READ DANIEL 9:3–19 ——————————

Daniel might not have been guilty of the trespasses for which he repented on behalf of his people. Think about that. He is not crying out to God on his own behalf but rather as a representative of the people. Perhaps you've heard the saying, "Not my monkeys, not my circus," or "It's not my problem." There is a time for us to say, "Not my sin, not my mistakes." Boundary keeping is important. But there also comes a time when our relative innocence coupled with our affiliation with a certain group of people gives us the credibility to be the advocate on behalf of the guilty. In fact, in the prophetic book of Joel, we read of how the priests are expected to cry out for mercy on behalf of the people (Joel 2:17). We can think of how Abraham did this for the people of the land in which his nephew Lot lived (Genesis 18:20–33). And of course, we shouldn't forget the life-changing moment when Jesus took upon himself the sins of the world (1 Peter 2:21–25).

So, we find Daniel fasting with sackcloth and ashes. In his doing so, we see him walking in a long tradition of corporate repentance. Just as the people and the king of Nineveh together declared a community fast, requiring all people and animals within the country to turn away from evil and to stop doing wrong (Jonah 3:1–10), Daniel stands in as a voice recognizing his own community's unmet need to fast and repent.

This time of fasting is different from the prior fast, the one offered by the people of Israel at the destruction of Jerusalem, as recorded in the book of Lamentations. They fasted as an expression of their grief at the great loss of life, home, Temple, and their sense of connection with a God who comforts. Here Daniel fasts as an expression of grief over the people's sin and a desire to understand the mysteries of God.

Crying out for God to hear, forgive, listen, and act, Daniel intercedes for the people. He does this by recognizing God's awesomeness and appealing to God's good identity and promises. He confesses that the people have

217

sinned and have incurred public shame. He mourns their deaf ears toward the words of the prophets. He recognizes that this time of diaspora is a consequence of breaking the covenant with God. He draws a contrast between the people's disobedience, disloyalty, and shame and God's compassion and forgiveness. Then he asks God to show them the same mercy that God previously showed Israel when they were enslaved in Egypt. They cannot save themselves. Importantly, Daniel makes request for the restoration of Jerusalem and God's sanctuary there for God's glory.

TIME OF REFLECTION

Go Deeper: Psalm 137 or Jeremiah 7

Read Jeremiah 7:16. Daniel seems to understand that a time was set for his people's punishment and a time has come for their repentance and return. He may also have a sense that if they don't turn back toward God, their punishment could be extended (Numbers 13 and 14).* As a prophet and a student of history, he understands there is "a time for every activity under heaven" (Ecclesiastes 3:1). Where in your life do you need to wait and trust God's timing?

Where in your life might God be waiting for you to act?

Where does public shame have a place in calling a group of people to repentance?

---

* After fleeing Egypt, when the Hebrew people made it to the edge of the Promised Land, they were not allowed to enter because they didn't believe that God would make them successful. Due to their lack of faith and complaints against God, they were punished with wandering in the desert until that generation passed. So, even though they had just been delivered from Egypt, they were not yet allowed to enter the Promised Land due to their sin. See Numbers 13 and 14.

How might God be calling you to be a representative of your people? Is it to speak to them or to speak on their behalf?

Is there any part of Daniel's prayer that you need to pray?

DANIEL AS BELOVED

——— READ DANIEL 9:20–23 ———

Sometimes, it seems like it takes forever for God to answer our prayers. We feel like the widow who continually went before the judge pleading for justice, only to be turned down again and again until one day, the judge concedes because of her persistence (Luke 18:1–8). And then there are the other times when, at the moment we begin to pray, God begins to send a response and it is fully realized while we are still praying. Daniel has likely experienced both types of prayers. But here in this passage, he not only receives a response, but he also receives the blessing of affirmation—you who sought understanding are beloved by God!

Dwell in that thought for a moment. Whatever God's response is going to be, the first message that God seems to desire for Daniel to know is that God has heard him and that he is treasured. Daniel is primarily interceding for others, yet God wants Daniel to know that Daniel matters to God.

As I write this, I am preparing a small-group study on kindness. The study begins by looking at the loving-kindness of God (Genesis 1:27; Titus 3:4–6; Nehemiah 9:17; Psalm 63:3). Sometimes we forget to remember that God is kind. This is especially challenging to remember when reading apocalyptic texts that speak of judgment, but we must remember the thousands of years of mercy that came prior and that the judgment is mercy for those who, like the persistent widow, are waiting for the judge to rule and make things right.

TIME OF REFLECTION

Go Deeper: Titus 3:4–7

Who or what is precious or treasured in your eyes? Why?

The Hebrew word " הֶּדְמָה chemdâh"[7] identifies Daniel as precious / desired / a delight in God's eyes. Do you see yourself as someone who is precious, desired, and a delight in God's eyes? Why or why not?

If you doubt that you are precious in God's eyes, how might that change?

Daniel had been reflecting upon how he and his people had wronged God. Imagine what Daniel's mindset had been at this moment. How does the affirmation "You are beloved by God" stand out in this moment? How might Daniel have experienced these words?

THE MESSAGE

What takes place during the seventy weeks? It seems that although Daniel has interpreted Jeremiah's prophecy to be speaking of the Babylonian captivity, perhaps the message shared by Gabriel is about something more, another time after Daniel. The angel is pushing Daniel to look beyond his present circumstances to the bigger picture of God's relationship with humanity. How mysterious these words must have sounded to a BC (Before Christ) man! I'm sure he has no clue that the answer he receives from God will still be read and studied and analyzed 1,500 years later. So often this seems to be God's response to our prayers: "Listen, child, this isn't about you. You are loved, but there is a bigger picture at play." So, what do these words mean for those of us living in AD (anno Domini / in the year of our Lord)?

Daniel's prayer is requesting forgiveness and restoration; God's response is about the same, just for another time. When we come to the gospel story, in what is considered by most scholars to be the first written gospel, the book of Mark, we are greeted with these words from Jesus: "The time is fulfilled, and the kingdom of God has come near. Repent and believe the good news!" (Mark 1:15). The first chapter of Mark introduces Jesus as the one who forgives sins, baptizes with the Holy Spirit, is God's "beloved son," is served by angels, calls disciples from amongst Israel, teaches with Divine authority in the synagogue, drives out unclean spirits, heals the sick, and lives a life of private twilight prayer. He does all of this while being the righteous and anointed (Luke 4:16–21) faithful fulfillment of the law and the prophets (Matthew 5:17). We see an echo of Daniel in our Savior Jesus, as they are both beloved, served by angels, and called to speak on behalf of God's Spirit to both Israel and those outside of Israel. But unlike Daniel, Jesus has the power and authority of being the Divinity as God's Son.

Daniel understands time in exile to be the reparations of sin. He is waiting in hope for the restoration of Israel. Jesus comes to be that reparation and to make a way for faith and mercy for all people. He seals up what was and, building upon Abraham's faith, confirms the patriarch's faith with something new, the Church.

Yet, Israel still waits in expectation for their Messiah to come, even though he has already arrived. But he will come again, and the lost sheep of Israel will be gathered and Israel will be restored (Jeremiah 31:10–12; Romans 9–11).

TIME OF REFLECTION

Go Deeper: Jeremiah 31

How do you see Jesus restraining sin, atoning for iniquity, bringing about everlasting righteousness, sealing up vision and prophecy, and being anointed as the Most Holy, thus fulfilling this prophecy?

Were seventy years in the diaspora enough to break the pattern of sin and unfaithfulness found amongst the people?

How then is Jesus the answer to Daniel's prayer?

THE TIMELINE

READ DANIEL 9:25–27

To begin, I highly recommend reading this passage from more than one translation of the Bible. In doing so, you'll discover that several questions are raised by this passage when it comes to understanding the timeline it proposes.

First, three periods of time are named that add up to seventy: seven, sixty-two, and one. Are these time periods overlapping, consecutive, or consecutive with gaps? Second, how is one to interpret the length of time represented by the word "weeks" or "sevens"? These questions lead to even more questions.

Let's start with the first. Daniel is expecting, in the near future, a decree for his people to return to rebuild the Temple. Yet, we know that this rebuilt Temple, known as the Second Temple, was destroyed in 70 AD. Perhaps the separation of the seven and sixty-two represent a hesitation or pause in the timeline between the two time periods. So, when we look at this time schedule, does the first seven begin after the first call to rebuild and the sixty-two begin after a future call to rebuild?* Or does the sixty-two begin immediately following the completion of the first seven, such that the sixty-two represent the time that this Second Temple stands for all to see? Or could both the seven and the sixty-two weeks begin from the same starting date such that when the first seven are complete, only fifty-five years remain of the sixty-two?

The Jewish Study Bible, Tanakh translation, offers a clear translation and with it an interpretation of this passage. It reads,

> "You must know and understand: From the issuance of the word
> to restore and rebuild Jerusalem until the [time of the] anointed
> leader is seven weeks; and for sixty-two weeks it will be rebuilt,

---

* Some have seen this fulfillment in Israel's application to be recognized as an independent nation-state by the United Nations in 1948, in Israel reclaiming Jerusalem in 1967, or in Israel's legal proclamation of ownership of Jerusalem in 1980.

square and moat, but in a time of distress. And after those sixty-two weeks, the anointed one will disappear and vanish." (Daniel 9:25–26a JSB)

An alternative reading is offered by the New American Standard Bible:

> "So you are to know and discern *that* from the issuing of a decree to restore and rebuild Jerusalem until Messiah the Prince *there will be* seven weeks and sixty-two weeks; it will be built again, with plaza and moat, even in times of distress.
>
> Then after the sixty-two weeks the Messiah will be cut off and have nothing, and the people of the prince who is to come will destroy the city and the sanctuary." (Dan. 9:25–26a NASB)

How we talk about this division of time is correlated with how we think of the anointed one mentioned within it. Does the awaiting of the Anointed One (the Hebrew word here is transliterated as "Messiah") refer to the time leading up to the anointing of a priest or king who will rule once Jerusalem is reestablished, or to the Messiah's first coming as Jesus of Nazareth, or does it refer to a still much-awaited apocalyptic appearance of the Messiah? Some argue that this refers to two[8] or three[9] different anointed ones, perhaps the first two being a type of messiah pointing to the later arrival of The Messiah. Some common historical interpretations identify Zerubbabel, the high priest Joshua,* the high priest Onias III, and Judas Maccabeus as anointed ones fulfilling this text. In fact, seven years passed between the removal of Onias III by Antiochus and the leadership of Judas Maccabeus.[10] On the other hand, a group of Christian theologians known as Dispensationalists prominently argue that the seven plus sixty-two occur sequentially between the time of the decree to rebuild Jerusalem (Nehemiah 2:1–8) and Jesus's triumphal entry into Jerusalem.[11] Or is it possible that we might be living in the sixty-two weeks now as we wait for Christ to be cut off?

---

* The prophet Zechariah refers to Joshua and Zerubbabel as the two anointed ones (Zechariah 4:14). But still others argue that Judas Maccabeus was the final fulfillment.

Second, how do we understand the quantity represented by the units of time labeled as "weeks"? Could each unit represent one generation, which would be estimated to be about seventy years? This means multiplying seven times seventy years in the first instance, sixty-two times seventy years in the second, and interpreting the last week as one generation as well. This leads to a total of 4,900 years. Or do we return to a Pentateuch emphasis, in which a week is completed by a Sabbath rest? Thus, six days conclude with a seventh day of rest, then six years are completed with a seventh year of rest, and seven sabbaths of years, or seven times seven, so forty-nine years conclude with the fiftieth year of rest known as the Jubilee (Leviticus 25:1–34).* Thus, if one "week" equals seven sabbaths of years (or fifty years), then seventy sabbaths of years totals 3,500 years. Some ancient commentators saw the math as seventy times seven (the number seven representing a week)[12] or as more modern writers have explained, "70 periods of seven, or 490 years."[13] Similarly, the word "week" could represent a single year or a group of seven years, such that seven weeks is forty-nine years and sixty-two weeks is 483 years.[14] Then again, we could interpret a week as an actual literal week.

A variety of attempts have been made to make this prophecy tangible. Ancient commentators tried to make the 490 years match with the return from Babylon to the much later Roman persecution of the new Christians, starting with the crucifixion of Jesus and continuing, as recorded in the book of Acts.[15] Some have identified the first seven weeks as being the time it takes to rebuild the Temple at the end of the Babylonian captivity. In 2 Chronicles 36:20–23, we read of Cyrus's 538 BC[16] proclamation to rebuild the Jerusalem Temple, but after an interruption in the project (Ezra 4:23–24) and then the intervention of Darius around 515 BC,[17] the work continues as described in the books of Ezra and Nehemiah, with its dedication approximately seventy years later, sometime after 444 BC.[18] The sixty-two weeks (or 434 years) have been correlated with the time after the Temple is complete up until the birth of Christ, sometime between 6 BC and 1 AD. Then, if the final week starts with the incarnation of Christ (birth of Jesus), mid-week, around 33 AD, we

---

* Yes, this is how the math is factored. So, it isn't six sabbaths of years, but seven sabbaths of years because the focus isn't on the last unit of sabbaths of years but on the actual year that completes the whole.

see the cutting off of Christ at his crucifixion for the benefit of others. Then, this week concludes with Titus destroying the Temple and murdering the people in 70 AD.[19] This interpretation sees the Messiah as the active, positive agent in "cutting off" and bringing an end to sacrifice, rather than the destroyer being the harmful, active agent ending the worship of God, unless one sees Titus as the destroyer.

Another way is to see Antiochus IV, who we read about previously, as the key player who murders the high priest Onias III in 171 BC and desecrates the Temple in 167 BC.[20] With this interpretation, seventy weeks are seen to pass between the beginning of the deportation and the much later cleansing of the rebuilt Temple by Judas Maccabeus.[21]

So much of contemporary interpretation wants to read this passage as describing events that have already taken place. We try to match the time frame with significant historical dates that we know. But what if the answer to Daniel's prayer isn't about the return from Babylon or the first redemptive coming of the Christ but actually about a future time in which the Reign of God is established more tangibly than how it has been established thus far in Israel or the Church? What if this vision remains to be fulfilled? Or what if we are still in the middle of its fulfillment? Or what if it is both—it has been fulfilled and it will be fulfilled?

For Daniel, this vision promised him that Jerusalem would be rebuilt, but during troublesome times; that there would be an Anointed Prince who would arise, but at some point, either he or the current religious system would be cut off; and that there would be yet another moment in which the Temple and city would be desolated, but the desolator would be destroyed.

In devotional day 84, we will return to both this last verse and Daniel 8:11–14, which carry a similar sentiment, when we look into the final four verses of Daniel and how Jesus interpreted Daniel's words regarding the "abomination of desolation."

TIME OF REFLECTION

Go Deeper: 2 Chronicles 36:20–21

How do you interpret "Anointed One"? What informs your interpretation? The book of Daniel? The Bible as a whole? Some other source?

Take time to research the year of Jubilee. When did this last take place? When is it expected to happen again? What was the biblical significance of the Jubilee year?

When Peter asked Jesus, "How many times shall I forgive my brother or sister who sins against me?" (Matthew 18:21), Jesus responded, "seventy times seven" (Matt. 18:22). How do you see God's forgiveness playing out over these "seventy times seven" years prophesied in Daniel? And how is this an answer to Daniel's prayer?

What are the strengths and weaknesses of the various interpretations of this passage?

THE FAST

As the people return to their Promised Land after seventy years in exile, they ask whether they should keep the fast that they have kept during their time away. The prophet Zechariah questions whether the fast they had kept was really for God or if it was for themselves. Had they really changed from the unrepentant people who they were prior to the exile?

The Lord challenges them through Zechariah: "Make fair decisions. Show faithful love and compassion to one another. Do not oppress the widow or the fatherless, the resident alien or the poor, and do not plot evil in your hearts against one another" (Zechariah 7:9–10). If they had previously listened to and obeyed this request from God, they may not have ended up in captivity in foreign lands. Their land wouldn't have been left in desolation. So, now that they are returning, will they listen to God?

TIME OF REFLECTION

Go Deeper: Isaiah 58

Look around you at your church and your culture. Do you, your church, and your culture obediently respond to God's command to care for the people who are vulnerable around you?

These instructions given through Zechariah seem so simple and straightforward, but they aren't always that easy for us to follow. Why?

How can you follow Christ's example and the instructions of God in being just, showing compassion, welcoming the oppressed, and not plotting evil against another person?

ACTION

This series of devotionals was originally written as the Christian liturgical season of Lent approached. This is a somber time period for drawing near to God for the forty days plus Sundays that lead up to the great celebration of Easter. How might the habit of following an annually cyclical pattern of holy days guide one's faith? Spend time today reflecting upon your patterns of repentance and celebration and how your rhythm of life either honors, is neutral toward, ignores, or dishonors God. What might you change going forward? Spend time in prayer talking to God about what you have discovered.

DANIEL 6

(And now we return to Chapter 6.)

THE LION'S DEN

THE GOOD PERSON

———— READ DANIEL 6:1–5 ————

Why are goodness, integrity, and achievement so offensive to some? Is it because the right living of the righteous makes our own vulnerabilities, foibles, and sins seem all that more pressing? Why do we pressure the good to not be so good? We mock them. We even correct them for their goodness. It is as if we can't just let them be a role model for the rest of us to respect, admire, and desire to follow. We inadvertently push these people, who make us all better, into the shadows, where they are appreciated* but for which the larger society will miss out.

At the beginning of this story, we are reminded again of how the Spirit of God dwells within and guides Daniel with wisdom and in righteousness. As a result, King Darius considers putting him in charge of the entire kingdom. It reminds me of how we anticipate the day in which a good ruler with a moral compass and wisdom will step up and be in charge. A day that Daniel has previously prophesied will come in the reign of God's saints and the "Son of Man."

It is almost as if Daniel, in this story, embodies what might take place when that day comes. When no fault can be found in that longed-for leader . . . when the people are acting in ways that are good and just . . . those who can't handle it for whatever reason will launch an attack on that leader and those people's strengths: their faith and commitment to God's law. They will attempt to redefine this strength as a weakness, not knowing that what God defines as good and just cannot be overturned.

---

* Those living in the shadows are already aware of their marginalization and, as a result, can appreciate the love and kindness that is shown to them by these righteous souls who are ignored or displaced by broader society.

This is the thing, though: God has promised prosperity* and success to those who obey His law.[1] God has committed to provide for those who are righteous and humble in heart. Instead of turning against those who model purity of heart, kindness, and the fruit of the Spirit spoken of in Galatians 5, let's instead learn from them. Let us see how God's law does not punish us but instead gives us hope. Let us find the wisdom that is a light that comes from God's direction. Let us honor those who can show us the path to walk in by following in their footsteps.

---

* I am not advocating for a health and wealth prosperity gospel here. Good people do get sick and even die. Good people can be economically poor. The faithful do not always have the desires of their heart met, or at least not in the way that they imagined. Hebrews 11 reminds us that not every biblical character got to see their promise fulfilled. Other people's sin can get in the way of our receiving God's provisions. But there is an overall sense that those who live for God experience a form of blessedness that is not experienced apart from God. Humans made Daniel's life difficult, and yet God provided for him within that context. Maybe a better word here would be that those who faithfully obey "thrive."

TIME OF REFLECTION

Go Deeper: Joshua 1:6–9; Ezekiel 14:12–14, 19–20; 2 Timothy 3:12

Who in your life reminds you of Daniel?

When was the last time you told this person what you appreciate about them?

How have you dismissed someone's goodness as naïve, when in actuality, their goodness showed maturity or wisdom?

How might you go about making goodness popular?

THE SETUP

— READ DANIEL 6:6–17 —

Remember that Daniel is a foreigner, a displaced person living in a land that is not his own. He was brought here as a captive. And the native people with whom he lives are also a colonized people. He is a religious and ethnic minority. Some might even say he is the token Hebrew leader, well-deserving of his rank but not given the respect by his colleagues that he deserves. It is in this context that we read this chapter's account of what went down when his colleagues contrived his demise.

What Daniel's colleagues request of the king is something they can obey, but they know Daniel cannot. It is targeted legislation. And they lie in wait, watching carefully for Daniel to do what he always does: kneel in prayer at his window facing his homeland and the place that honors the name of the Holy One, Jerusalem. Daniel continually chooses to worship God; this is the one place he is unwilling to compromise as a Hebrew man in a foreign land. And when the king is confronted with the accusation against his most trusted companion, he realizes with deep regret what he has done. But for the king to show integrity, as Daniel models integrity, he must uphold the law, even if it means death to his friend.

Like many in modern days who have searched the law, even making final-hour death penalty appeals for those awaiting execution, the king searches the law until taunted by his subordinates, "Know, O king, that *it is* the law of the Medes and Persians that no decree or statute which the king establishes may be changed."[2] And so with great regret, Darius gives the command for Daniel to go through a trial by ordeal. He commands Daniel to be thrown into the pit of lions, saying, "Your God, whom you serve continually will deliver you."[3]

With those words, I am sure Daniel remembers his friends Shadrach, Meshach, and Abednego, and their preservation through the fiery furnace. I am sure Daniel remembers how, when they first arrived in Babylon, God paved the way for them to eat kosher, even when it was offensive. I am sure

Daniel remembers how when all the wise men were threatened with death if they could not identify what Neb had dreamt and interpret it, God supplied young Daniel with both the dream and its interpretation. And I am sure Daniel remembers the apocalyptic dreams he had that both made him tremble and gave him hope. It is these memories that I am sure faithful and mature Daniel recalls as yet another king stumbles while saying, "May your God save you."

TIME OF REFLECTION

Go Deeper: 1 Kings 8:27–30

In spring 2020, in many parts of the world, governments passed legislation that made it illegal to assemble. The stated purpose of these laws was to decrease the spread of the virus known as COVID-19. These laws covered many types of assembly, including concerts, theaters, restaurants, and corporate worship. Some worshippers claimed these laws were religious persecution and thus could be disobeyed for the purpose of gathering to worship. Others recognized them as more generally applied laws that were to be obeyed and subsequently found new ways to worship. In the book of Daniel, we have witnessed Daniel model a unique balance of both assimilating with the prevailing culture and upholding the distinct boundaries of his religious way of life. How do you think Daniel would have practiced his faith in the context of laws forbidding all forms of assembly?

What are the non-negotiables of the *practice* of your faith?

RELIGIOUS PERSECUTION

———————— READ DANIEL 6:10–13 ————————

A remnant. The existence of a group of people who remain from a greater whole is a key theological concept in biblical history. God always preserves a remnant of God's people. Whether Noah and his wife and children being saved from the global flood (Genesis 6:5–8, 7:1, 8:15–22) or Daniel and his colleagues residing as part of the diaspora in Babylon (Daniel 1:1–4), there always is and always will be a continuance of God's people.

That is not to say that God's people won't experience religious persecution. When I was in seminary, we learned that during the latter part of the Reformation, *Foxe's Book of Martyrs* was chained to pulpits and read from on a regular basis.[4] This chronicle of the history of religious persecution against followers of Christ served as a reminder to those who heard excerpts of it that persecution would come and that we, as believers, were called to persevere despite the cost of remaining faithful. In more contemporary times, organizations like Open Doors, Operation World, and Voice of the Martyrs have tracked the rise and fall of persecution against Christians in locales around the world.

And none of us should be naïve to the evil that has been targeted against our Jewish brothers and sisters of faith throughout the ages. Antisemitism[*] is real and continues to threaten God's people. Whether it is a direct violent attack, a denial of historical events, a pressure to "fit in," or a subtle "othering" or "stereotyping," it is something for which we should stand up and speak against when we see it taking place.

After the time of Daniel, a young Jewish woman, Esther, was chosen to be queen of Persia. While queen, a man named Haman became jealous and hateful toward her people, the Jewish community, and as a result convinced the king to issue a decree that authorized the destruction of this people group.

---

[*] To see a working definition of antisemitism that is used internationally at the time of the writing of this book, visit https://www.state.gov/defining-antisemitism/ or look up the International Holocaust Remembrance Alliance and the May 26, 2016, plenary in Bucharest.

He argued that they were separatists who followed a different code of law than what was set by the king, so they shouldn't be tolerated (Esther 3:1–9). Despite Haman's attempts to destroy God's people, God had already put Esther in a place of influence where she could wisely speak on her people's behalf and save them (Est. 8:3–14). In a similar way, we are called to persevere in our faith despite any persecution we may face. We are to stand up, speak on behalf of, and defend those who are persecuted.

TIME OF REFLECTION

Go Deeper: Esther

Is it important to remember the stories of those who are persecuted or martyred for their faith? Why? What can we learn from these folks? How might we preserve their stories?

Where are God's people presently being persecuted for their faith?

Consider the following statement: Targeted violent attacks on [enter name of ethnic, racial, or religious community]'s place of worship, commerce, education, and living should be condemned. Does whether you agree or disagree with the statement change depending upon who you put in the bracket?

Are you more willing to support targeted violence during times of war? If so, why? How do you see people using war as a reason to justify the persecution of the innocent?

Do groups of people have the right to hold to a distinct value system that may be different than the accepted value system of a nation? Why or why not?

A LESSON FOR A KING

—————————— READ DANIEL 6:18–28 ——————————

This story isn't about Daniel. We often identify it as the story of "Daniel in the Lion's Den." But once again, we find that in Daniel's interactions with the kings of his day, it is all about the king coming to recognize the God of the Hebrews as the God of all people, including heads of state. Did you notice that King Darius is the main character? What did the king do while Daniel was in the den with the lions? He didn't sleep. He sat in silence. He fasted and prayed. And as soon as he was legally able, at the rise of the morning sun, he went to check on Daniel. And the question he poses is, "Has your God been able to deliver you?" He recognizes that the only way Daniel possibly could be alive this next day is if Daniel's God intervened.

The response he receives is the one that confirms to Darius that yes, indeed, this is a God in whom he can put his trust. Daniel first explains that God sent an angel to close the lions' mouths. Next, he explains that God had found Daniel innocent before God of breaking the first two commandments (Exodus 20:1–4). He had not bowed down before anyone other than God. He was also innocent before the king, for he had not wronged the governing authority over him. Thus, he was innocent of the punishment before him. And so there can be no doubt in the reader's mind of Daniel's assessment of the situation, when Darius throws Daniel's accusers into the den, the hungry and veracious lions consume them while they are still in the air. Daniel was saved "because he believed in his God."[5]

The first half of the book of Daniel, the part focused on the kings, ends with King Darius offering a very different edict from the first one he issued, a clear reversal of course. He announces that the God of Daniel is the Living God, whose kingdom will never be destroyed, who reveals Himself through signs and wonders, and that all people everywhere should fear this God.

TIME OF REFLECTION

Go Deeper: Romans 15:1–13

Some people are very uncomfortable with a head of state proclaiming one god as the ultimate god who is to be respected by all. Why does this make people, including perhaps yourself, uncomfortable?

Is there a difference between a head of state proclaiming one god as God and a head of state telling people how they are to worship that god? Why or why not?

Is there a god worthy of this proclamation by a head of state?

How would this work out if the head of your government made the statement Darius is recorded as making in Daniel 6:25–27?

ACTION

---------- RE-READ DANIEL 6 ----------

What is your plan? Whether we experience a home fire, a natural disaster, a health incident, or a terrorist attack, those who are prepared are better able to respond. Have you decided how you will respond if you must choose between your faith and [fill in the blank]? Daniel was clearly prepared to respond. In verse 23, we are told that Daniel "trusted in his God." He went home and he prayed as he had always prayed. What is your plan?

DANIEL 10

(And now for the final three chapters of Daniel ...)

ENCOUNTERS

LAYERS OF A MASTERPIECE

———————— READ DANIEL 10–12 ————————

We've been watching an artist at work, creating layer upon layer of a masterpiece, beginning with the broad strokes of the background with the dream of the statue and the vision of the beasts and now adding the details of the foreground. Details that are so explicit that this prophecy is entirely testable in its fulfillment. When it takes place, the watchful observer and student who holds the Bible in one hand and a news source in the other will know that the time is here and now. Things that seem vague in this moment will likely gain clarity. The illogical will appear sensical. The message will be unveiled before their very eyes. And so we, too, must be alert, for the time is near.

As I've been journeying through the book of Daniel these last two years, the similarities between historical events and present moments have been uncanny. As I enter this last stage of writing and this last vision, I have some trepidation. What if I am able to understand what I am about to read with the clarity of someone living within the painting, recognizing the details closest to me and having a sense that the broader strokes are part of my own environment? What if the time is now?

TIME OF REFLECTION

Go Deeper: 2 Timothy 3:1–4:8; 2 Corinthians 5:20–7:1; Romans 13:11

As you have read through the book of Daniel thus far, have there been any stories that have felt uncannily familiar to you? If so, how did you deal with those similarities?

What currently points your attention to God as Mysterious Other intimately engaged in the affairs of humanity?

Do you have a sense that the time is now? Or that the time is near? Or is it your view that all we have read about has already passed? Or that the fulfillment is still yet to be discovered in an unknown but somewhat predictable future? Or is it some combination of these? How do you interpret these texts in comparison to your contemporary moment?

Could it be possible to live through prophesied events and miss them? Perhaps they appear differently than we expect. What evidence do you have to support your thoughts on this? What role does humility (in contrast to arrogance) play in accurately witnessing and recognizing fulfillment?

EXPERIENCE THE VISION

—————————— READ DANIEL 10:1, 7–11, 15–19; 12:9, 13 ——————————

The introduction to this last vision invites us back into the first chapter of Daniel, where we learned that Daniel was taken from Jerusalem to Babylon against his will and that his time in Babylon would last until the first year of King Cyrus. We are reminded that Daniel was given a new Babylonian name and called into the service of these foreign Gentile kings. In those early days, he established himself and showed his faithfulness by keeping a simplified kosher diet, and God rewarded him for it with knowledge, understanding, and the ability to interpret visions. Now, seventy-plus years later, he is an old man who has enjoyed the finer wines, meats, and even lotions of wealth, but he has decided once again to fast. This time, the fast is much longer, and he is motivated either by a desire to receive a revelation from God or by his desire to better understand one already received. Aspects of this process seem similar to a man on his deathbed: a reduced diet, weakness, and difficulty breathing. As a pastor, I have observed that as people near their last days, they are sometimes more attuned to "last things" (eschatological possibilities). That being said, this business of receiving visions and encountering God can be a tiring affair. But Daniel is given strength and told that when his time comes, he will rest, and then at the *very end*, he will rise and receive an inheritance.

As you re-read these verses, take time to experience the vision with Daniel. Imagine yourself falling prostrate face-first to the ground in reverence of God. Feel the weakness in your body as you are overwhelmed by the experience. Imagine the holy hand that touches first, perhaps, your shoulders and then your lips. Feel your body tremble. Listen to his voice and the words he speaks. Hold dearly to the instruction, "Peace be with you; take courage and be courageous!"[1]

Wonder for a while about who this "one with a human appearance"[2] might be. Is it the "Son of Man" who appeared in a previous vision? (Daniel 7:13).

Or perhaps it is the angel Gabriel who had previously appeared to Daniel (Dan. 8:15). What does it mean that this one touching him appeared in the likeness of the son of Adam ("ben adam")? Could these words be a reminder that in Adam we all died, but in Christ we gain life? (Romans 5:12–15, 19, 6:12). Who is this being who touches Daniel and both causes him to tremble and gives him peace?

TIME OF REFLECTION

Go Deeper: Isaiah 6:6–8; Ezekiel 1:1–2:2

Why might prophetic "end times" affairs be important to people as they are nearing death?

How do you imagine yourself responding if your room were to become full of an otherworldly light, and either the glorified Messiah or an angel appeared to you?

What does your imagined response tell you about your belief regarding the character and identity of God?

How does your imagined response compare to the experiences of those in the Bible who had such encounters?

THREE-WEEK FAST

READ DANIEL 10:2–3, 12, 14

I must admit that I have been cautious about preaching on fasting. Some readers may have astutely picked up my hesitation and wondered when I would invite the reader to follow the biblical example and fast.* Fasting is a common religious practice that is an important expression of faith, but I grew up in a culture in which young men lost and gained weight seemingly overnight to meet weight requirements for wrestling competitions, and young women interpreted "diet" to not mean the balance of foods one eats but instead the removal of foods and nutrition from one's diet for the misplaced hope of improving her appearance. Neither of which I believe are healthy practices. I am also aware of food deserts, as I once lived in an urban one, and consequently, I recognize there is a privilege that comes with the accessibility of food. All of these ideas are concerns of mine. But, a fast done properly, with a focus on God and guided by the wisdom of spiritual mentors and, if needed, medical professionals, offers much opportunity for spiritual blessing and breakthrough. It is a practice that most of us should try.

Some pastors have maneuvered around similar concerns by defining fasting as giving up a pleasure or a habit for a time rather than changing one's eating habits. Yet when the Bible speaks of a "fast," it is referring to a change in diet from physical nourishment to spiritual nourishment. While I have hesitations about this topic, I have also experienced food-related fasts focused on the seeking of God that have significantly impacted my life. I've had friends fast in my place when I couldn't fast for myself. I've set aside months at a time when I avoided pork and ocean bottom-feeders and removed products with certain ingredients from our home as an act of spiritual devotion. There have been times when I have sought God's wisdom and only eaten vegetables and fruit

---

* If you are interested in fasting, I suggest reading Richard J. Foster's chapter on this spiritual exercise in his book, *Celebration of Discipline: The Path to Spiritual Growth.* He provides helpful instruction on the "how to" of fasting.

and drank water. And yes, I have also practiced the day-long spiritual discipline of not eating and sometimes not drinking, supplementing what would have been my mealtime with the Word of God. Yet, in times when fasting from food would not have been healthy for me, I have instead intentionally set aside longer mealtimes to eat thoughtfully, to read Scripture, and to pray.

Biblically, fasting has been practiced for a variety of reasons. The more prominent has been as an act of repentance. It is a way of humbling ourselves before God and repenting of our self-reliance, arrogance, and sin. There are times we hear the call of Joel 2:12–13,

> "'Return to Me, with all your heart,
> And with fasting, weeping and mourning;
> And rend your heart and not your garments.'
> Now return to the LORD your God,
> For He is gracious and compassionate,
> Slow to anger, abounding in lovingkindness
> And relenting of evil." (NASB)

People have also fasted to prepare themselves for holy acts and encounters, such as Ezra and the Jewish people did as they prepared to return from Babylon to Israel to reestablish worship in the Temple of Jerusalem. They called on God to give them a safe journey there (Ezra 7–8).

Fasting is also a way of expressing commitment to God. It can be a step in holy dedication. It is a way to signify this is a time or person that is being set apart for God. An influential early church document, the *Didache*, directed people to fast in the days leading up to their Christian baptism and encouraged those who were to witness the baptism to fast as well.[3] The Anglican church has had a history of calling people to fast on Fridays, and this spiritual discipline was adopted by early followers of John Wesley, the founder of Methodism, who added a second day of fasting, Wednesday, to their religious practice.

Fasting can also be a response to an encounter with God. Following his own baptism, Jesus went into the desert to fast and pray for forty days (Matthew 3–4).* Fasting can be a means of seeking an encounter with God.

While there is a clear biblical and religious call to fasting, we hear God remind us that if we change our eating practices but do not change our attitude or behavior and do not focus on God through prayer or worship, our fast is just going through the motions. In Isaiah 58:3a, the question is raised, "Why have we fasted and You do not see?" (NASB). From the people's perspective, they had sought God and they had done what they thought was right, but God wanted something different from them. Isaiah 58:3b–4, 6–8 answers their questions:

> "Yet on the day of your fasting, you do as you please and
>   exploit all your workers.
>
> Your fasting ends in quarreling and strife, and in striking
>   each other with wicked fists.
>
> You cannot fast as you do today and expect your voice
>   to be heard on high …
>
> Is not this the kind of fasting I have chosen:
>   to loose the chains of injustice and untie the cords of the yoke,
>   to set the oppressed free and break every yoke?
>
> Is it not to share your food with the hungry and to provide the
>   poor wanderer with shelter—when you see the naked, to clothe
>   them, and not to turn away from your own flesh and blood?
>
> Then your light will break forth like the dawn, and your healing
>   will quickly appear; then your righteousness will go before you,
>   and the glory of the LORD will be your rear guard.

---

* If you are considering practicing a lengthy fast from food, please do your research first and consult with your doctor. Usually those who do longer fasts have had a few years of practice with shorter fasts. While we are to feast on the Word of God, God also designed our bodies to receive nourishment from food and water. Our bodies are God's temple, and as such, they are sacred. Don't forget, you are beautifully designed by God!

Then you will call, and the LORD will answer;
you will cry for help, and he will say: Here am I." (NIV)

Throughout this book, we have read again and again about people fasting, submitting themselves to God and one another while practicing a new form of God-reliant, trust-filled, self-control. Daniel sets aside rich foods and deprives his body of scented oils for three weeks as he mourns and seeks God's wisdom. This is a time of prayer. His attention is focused on God, and he is preparing himself to receive a response. The response he receives is a vision of the last days.

TIME OF REFLECTION

Go Deeper: Malachi

In the year 2020, many parts of our globe were forcefully pushed into a time of sabbath and fasting. I personally experienced this as an act of God's grace. Our world had been in this exponentially forward mode of being, and we had forgotten what it meant to rest and prioritize. Or at least here in the United States, that is how I experienced it.

Unfortunately, while some were able to be still and quiet and were given the opportunity to listen and learn from the silence and change of pace, others found themselves working more hours and harder and in less-favorable conditions. In the midst of this, realities of injustice came to the foreground. People gathered. They gathered to fast, and they expressed their fast in a variety of ways. For some it was prayer and worship, for others it was marching and singing, and still for others it was shared tears. And yet, somehow, I wonder if we missed the purpose of it all. Did we give up our fast prematurely? Did we miss some of the spiritual blessings because we weren't willing to recognize the goodness of God due to our pride? Was our repentance misdirected? How is it that our fast seemed to end with fists in the air rather than arms draped around each other's shoulders? The words of Joel 2 and Isaiah 58 at times have seemed to ring true. Which leads to today's questions:

In reflecting upon what you have learned about fasting and from the stories found in Daniel, how do you think God might be calling people to be in relationship with God and each other? In other words, what type of fast is God inviting us to enter?

How is this different from what you witness in the world today? Where have we failed in our fasting and in our enacting of God's ways?

What message do you think God has for the church today?

For you?

THE MAN DRESSED IN LINEN

———————— READ DANIEL 10:4–6, 12:5–7 ————————

Who Daniel encounters and what he learns in this last vision is so life-changing that Daniel does not want to forget the exact date or location of where it happened. I've had a spiritual encounter like that. Perhaps you have too? An encounter like this is not to be forgotten!

Daniel encounters the Son of Man not at a distance, like in the earlier vision of Daniel 7, but up close and personal. He experiences this Messiah as both magnificent and the glorified other and as the caring shepherd who knows and comforts his sheep by name. His description of the Son of Man becomes the church's understanding of the glorified Christ. We see it repeated in the vision that the beloved apostle John receives while on the island of Patmos in the Aegon Sea thirty to sixty years after the death and resurrection of Jesus (Revelation 1:9–20). Both Daniel and John relay the exceeding brightness of this man's face, his eyes that are like flames, his burnished bronze lower limbs, and his robust voice. They both fall before this One in human likeness, and both are told not to be afraid.*

The specificity of this last vision cannot be overlooked. Daniel relays in detail what he has seen and what he has learned. And we, the reader, are to take note: this is important!

---

* Often when a person bows before a messenger from God, they are told to rise because the person or angel is only the messenger, but here Daniel's adoration of the being in the vision is accepted. For this reason, I've interpreted the One in human likeness to be the resurrected Jesus. It could also be interpreted to be an angel.

TIME OF REFLECTION

Go Deeper: Revelation 1; Mark 13:21–27; Acts 9:1–12

Have you had an experience of sudden religious or spiritual awareness? Or have you encountered God in a life-changing or worldview-changing way? Take time to reflect upon this. If you haven't, do you know of anyone who has? What have you learned from hearing their story?

Having had an experience with God or the supernatural realm is much more common than what some people are willing to discuss. Whether it be angels, an unembodied voice that saved one's life, an out-of-body experience, or an encounter with Jesus, most people—whether they themselves, a close relative, or a close friend—have experienced an event like this. How might you go about opening up conversations about spiritual experiences with others?

Part of faith-filled spirituality is a willingness to be alert to the Divine in the everyday. This can be expressed by reading the Bible while listening for the Spirit to speak, admiring the beauty of Creation or the miracle of the human body, being attentive to thematic symbols or patterns in life, or even appreciating a social exchange with another human. Some even ask, "How did I encounter God today?" Do you live your life in a way that you are attentive to the Divine or at least willing to hear from God if God wanted to speak to you?

ANGELS FIGHTING IN HUMAN BATTLES

—— READ DANIEL 10:13, 10:20–11:1, 12:1 ——

Then war broke out in heaven. Michael and his angels fought against the dragon ['Satan, who leads the world astray'], and the dragon and his angels fought back" (NIV). These words from Revelation 12:7 (and 12:9 in brackets) are not often preached upon, or at least not in the circles in which I walk. We tend not to focus on the details of the spiritual realm. Yet, to read Daniel 10, and perhaps even to understand the vision of Daniel 10–12, we must pause for a moment and recognize that the physical realm isn't all of reality. There is a spiritual realm too. And what happens in each of these two realms impacts the other; they are interconnected.

In the Old Testament, we read of angel armies going out before Israel to fight on Israel's behalf. The famous King David hears "the sound of marching in the tops of the poplar trees" (2 Samuel 5:24a NIV) as the angelic army goes before them to defeat the Philistines (2 Sam. 5:17–25). Hezekiah, another king of Israel, calls on God for help when threatened by Sennacherib, king of the violent Assyrians. God responds by sending an angel to kill 185,000 Assyrian soldiers posed for war (2 Kings 19). In another situation (2 Kings 6:8–23), God reveals to Elisha, the prophet, the movements of Israel's enemy Aram so they can avoid crossing the Arameans' path. When their paths do cross, Elisha tells his servant not to be worried, as he opens the servant's eyes to see the "hills full of horses and chariots of fire" (2 Kings 6:17b NIV).

In the last chapter of Ephesians, we learn that "our struggle is not against flesh and blood, but against the rulers, against the authorities, against the cosmic powers of this darkness, against evil, spiritual forces in the heavens" (Ephesians 6:12). We learned back in Isaiah 59 that we need someone to intercede on our behalf, and God does that for us. That is part of what makes it so amazing that Jesus accepted death by crucifixion. Jesus testified when

Judas betrayed him that he was able to call upon "more than twelve legions of angels" to intervene on his behalf, but Jesus didn't because what was to come was necessary to fulfill God's purposes (Matthew 26:52–54).

In today's reading, the illuminating man* is delayed in responding to Daniel's prayers due to a prince of Persia getting in his way. He requires the help of the guardian angel or "prince" of Israel, Michael, to get through. Later, we read of how this otherworldly being must return to fight against the prince of Persia. Daniel is told that when this being leaves, the prince of Greece will come.

The word "prince" has been interpreted as an angel that represents or governs over a boundaried nation, geographical region, political entity like a city,[4] or people group. Thus, as you read more of the details of this vision, you might see it as a spiritual battle taking place parallel to battles fought by human armies.[5] Early Christian commentators grappled with this by saying that each angel is commissioned with looking out for the best interest of those under its care and advocating on behalf of its nation. This resulted in angels with conflicting interests.[6] On the other hand, some modern thinkers name these angels who oppose Michael as "demons," as they are seen as following the ways of Satan instead of the ways of God.

Others have interpreted "prince" as the actual human king ruling over a nation. With this interpretation, a human king is getting in the way of a messenger sent by God, and the angel Michael must intervene.

---

* Earlier, I named the man in the vision as the Messiah. Here, I offer an alternative, a more vague interpretation, recognizing that there is disagreement about who is and how many are present in the vision.

TIME OF REFLECTION

Go Deeper: Matthew 18:10; Revelation 12

From Genesis to Revelation, angels play a prominent role. Yet in the contemporary Western narrative, the spiritual realm is portrayed in a fictitious manner. By mocking, imitating, and fictionalizing the spiritual realm, does the West do a disservice to itself? Why or why not?

How might the battles we struggle with in our human realm also need to be fought in the spiritual realm? What role does prayer play in fighting our battles? Does prayer make a difference?

How would you compare the angelic realm and the human realm? For example, how do they each relate to time? Space? God?

ACTION

---- READ DANIEL 10 ----

You've read ten chapters of the book of Daniel. You've read about history, culture, symbolism, interpretation, visions, and dreams. Your mind and your heart have been challenged to go deeper into the biblical text and in your relationship with God. You have likely encountered God in the text of Daniel. Take time today to reflect upon how you have changed because of this encounter. Consider how God might be calling you to respond.

DANIEL 11

PROPHETIC DETAILS

KINGS OF PERSIA

———————————— READ DANIEL 11:1–4 ————————————

This prophecy begins by telling of six kings of an undivided Persia, the
fifth being richer than the three prior and using that wealth to gain power,
which is then used to stir the people against Greece. The final unrestrained
warrior king expands the kingdom significantly, but his rule is short, as the
realm is quickly divided into the northern kingdom, the southern kingdom,
and at least two other kingdoms.

Historians can connect much of the specificities of Daniel 11 with historical events that took place between King Cambyses of 530 BC (Daniel 11:2)
and the Maccabean "helpers" of the 160s BC (Dan. 11:34) who respond to
the covenant-breaking master of intrigue, Antiochus Epiphanes.[1] Remember
that all we read is through the eyes of Israel and the impact world events have
on Israel. In Israel's history, this is the time of the restoration and rebuilding
of the Temple and Jerusalem. The proposed five kings of Persia are Darius the
Mede (Dan. 11:1)/Cyrus (Dan. 10:1), Cambyses, Pseudo-Smerdis (believed
to actually be the deceptive Gaumata), Darius I (Hystaspes), and Xerxes I
(Ahasuerus),[2] although there are other options, including recognizing Artax-
erxes instead of Pseudo-Smerdis.[3] It is agreed that the sixth king is Alexander
the Great, the goat of chapter 8 (Greece), who has now conquered the land
of the ram (Persia).

By interpreting the final ruler to be Alexander the Great, we can then
attempt to identify the northern and southern kingdoms. Remember, back
in chapter 7, we named the four generals of Alexander's kingdom: Ptolemy,
Seleucus, Antigonus, and Cassander (Antipater) or Alexander's brother Philip.
Thus all four kingdoms are in proximity to the Mediterranean Sea. Historians
have then interpreted the northern kingdom to be Syria (formerly Babylon:
Jeremiah 25:8–9), ruled by the Seleucids, and the southern kingdom to be
Egypt (including Israel), ruled by the Ptolemies.[4] Note that Egypt and Israel

shared many encounters in the Genesis narrative, as Abraham and his descendants traveled to and from these lands.

TIME OF REFLECTION

Go Deeper: Daniel 7–8

Is it important to recognize the historical fulfillment of biblical prophecy? Why or why not? What is the benefit or disservice of doing so?

How does context matter when reading a Bible verse or group of verses?

What type of context helps in understanding the meaning of a single verse?

THE POWERFUL DAUGHTER

———————————— READ DANIEL 11:5–9 ————————————

This next section reads as if it were a Shakespearean drama. The southern king's commander and then later daughter take center stage. The northern kingdom undermines this southern daughter, only to be undermined later by one of her relatives. The mentioning of a female character grabs our attention, as this is only the second woman mentioned in the book of Daniel.* As women, in a general sense, have not received the same notoriety in history as men, the fulfillment of this detail offers a distinctive prophetic marker. One may wonder, though, that because it is the story of a woman, perhaps its fulfillment will go unnoticed under the shroud of privacy or historical and news negligence. Or perhaps just the opposite: it will gain greater attention as a story of public interest.

Historically, the events described in this passage align with the life of a woman named Berenice and the events that led up to the third of five Syrian wars (all fought between the Seleucids and the Ptolemaics). This third war was fought between Berenice's brother Ptolemy III Euergetes (of the south) and Berenice's husband's ex-wife Laodice (of the north) and her family,[5] as led by her son Seleucus II Callinicus.[6] If the book of Daniel is understood to be written during the persecution of Israel by Antiochus IV Epiphanes, and not a couple centuries earlier,† this story acts as a reminder of the history of the northern Seleucid dynasty,[7] of which Antiochus Epiphanes is a part. The retelling of this story would give further reason for the people of the time to dislike him.

This story begins with the end of Alexander the Great's rule and Ptolemy I Soter suggesting that the land be divided amongst the generals, with Ptolemy

---

* The queen during King Belshazzar's reign is the first woman mentioned in the book of Daniel. See Daniel 5:10–12. We also see a female character highlighted in the Greek translation of Daniel with the story of Susanna.

† Evidence from the Qumran caves supports an earlier date for Daniel than what is proposed here. Early dating places it in the sixth century BC, while later dating places the writing around the time of the Maccabees or later. Dr. Gerhard Hasel, "New Light on the Book of Daniel from the Dead Sea Scrolls," accessed on March 19, 2022, https://biblearchaeology.org/research/topics/ancient-manuscripts/3193-new-light-on-the-book-of-daniel-from-the-dead-sea-scrolls.

ruling over the Nile delta. From this he grew in power, establishing himself in Egypt and beyond. Following Alexander the Great's example, Ptolemy I Soter used marriages to build alliances. The dynasty of the Ptolemies would last until Roman rule.[8]

An interesting side note: according to the historical "Letter of Aristeas," Soter's son, Ptolemy II Philadelphus, initiated the writing of the Greek translation of the Old Testament known as the Septuagint.[9] This Ptolemy is the father of Berenice. Berenice, following the family pattern, married King Antiochus II Theos of the north in order to ensure peace between the two powers. But Antiochus had already been married, and his ex-wife, jealous of this arrangement, killed her ex-husband and his new wife.[10] Berenice's father also died around this same time, leading to his son Ptolemy III Euergetes taking rule and seeking retribution against Laodice.[11]

Stepping back from this historical scene, the Daniel narrative offers additional components to this prophecy that cannot be missed. As we read verse 6, this daughter seems an active agent in her own destiny, as there isn't a definitive mention of an arranged marriage. She is seen as one who is powerful, possibly within her own right, but then loses her power. I imagine her as an emperor's daughter who has been given authority to negotiate peace treaties or a wise woman who sees an opportunity to negotiate peace and grabs it.

We also cannot forget the commander or prince mentioned in verse 5. He emerges from within the southern kingdom as one of might who governs over an even greater kingdom. It is unclear if this commander becomes the ruler of the northern kingdom, as seen in Seleucus I Nicator, who defeated Antigonus and established the Seleucid dynasty;[12] if he becomes ruler of some other kingdom; if he simply has more influence within the kingdom than the king, as did the general Scopas;[13] or if this is the son of the southern king ruling in place of his father, as Ptolemy Philadelphus did.[14]

Next, we read of an alliance (or two).

Then in verses 7–9, we read of the daughter's successor who will be victorious over the northern king. Just as often takes place when one ruler conquers another in ancient times, the southern king will seize the carved idols and metallic wealth of the north and take it home with him.

TIME OF REFLECTION

Go Deeper: Judges 4–5; Acts 16:10–15

Throughout the book of Daniel, we read about the exchange of power. We see that human power is always moving between person and person, but God's power remains consistent. How is power being exchanged in today's narrative? How is it gained and lost?

What is the significance of this prophecy being fulfilled in such detail?

Is there any aspect of this prophecy that remains to be fulfilled?

WAR!

—— READ DANIEL 11:10–19 ——

War—it seems man's need to expand his territory has led to an endless cycle of battles across history and geography. Remember as you read this prophecy that Israel is caught between these two warring dynasties and the northern king's aggressive desire for more. We see the fulfillment of this in Israel shifting from the hands of the Ptolemies to the Seleucids around 200 BC.[15]

In verses 10–12, we learn of the northern aggression that sweeps through the region as far as they have fortresses. An infuriated south responds. There is a back-and-forth between the two, with many casualties, and Israel is caught in the middle. Historically this is interpreted as the battles that took place between Antiochus III (the Great) and Ptolemy IV Philopater.[16]

Then, in verses 13–16, we learn that the north takes a break from war to regroup, rebuilding their military and restocking their supplies. If there is a historical correlation here, Antiochus III is continuing to rule in the north with six-year-old Ptolemy V Epiphanes becoming ruler of the southern kingdom in 204 BC.[17]

The revelation to Daniel continues with others beginning to battle against the south, including rebellious people from Israel who are encouraged by a vision to do so. But none are like the north that gains dominance in a decisive battle against a southern city. The northern king advances, destroying everything in his path, including the elite military forces of the south and the "beautiful land," which likely refers to Israel.

In verses 17–18, we read of a possible treaty and an undesired arranged marriage, a reversal of the direction of the previous arrangement when the empowered woman from the south went to the north, as we read in verse 6. The woman in this arrangement is described as a "daughter of women" who is intended to undermine the country she is wed to but chooses to have no

part in doing the northern king's malicious bidding. "Daughter of women"*
stands out as it is parallel to Daniel's earlier use of the title "Son of man." It
could be interpreted as "her highness," as this is most understood to be a reference to Cleopatra, daughter of Antiochus III[18] and Laodice, wife of and
co-ruler with Ptolemy V. Epiphanes, and great-grandmother to the famous
Cleopatra.[19]

Finally, in verses 18–19, we read of the end of this northern king's reign,
as the taunting of a commander turns his attention back home, where he
stumbles and is no more. Historically, Antiochus III conquered several Greek
islands before being defeated by the Romans and then dies in 187 BC.[20]

---

* If one wants to take more freedom in interpreting *"baṭ 'iššâ"* in this passage, one may try to contemporize
it. It could be understood as referring to Jerusalem, the bride of Christ/the church, a stepdaughter, or one
could wrestle with questions about why we find the plural form instead of singular "woman." Is this prophetic of a time in which two women would mother a child together? Or perhaps this is used to draw attention to this woman as being the perfection of women, similarly to how "son of man" represents the perfection
of humanity in the Messiah.

TIME OF REFLECTION

Go Deeper: 2 Samuel 11:1

Why so great of detail? Why might this detailed vision have been revealed to Daniel?

Having survived one besiegement of Jerusalem and being hopeful of a return to this city, how might Daniel have heard the words of this prophecy? What is the message to Israel?

Who are the key characters in today's reading?

A DIFFERENT TYPE OF POWER

READ DANIEL 11:20–30

Sometimes, reading Daniel feels like reading an encrypted note. It is vague enough to not make sense and specific enough to gain credibility in its fulfillment. After the short-lived reign of a tax-collecting northern king, a new leader emerges whose rule is unexpected and consumes the remaining narrative of chapter 11. This is a man who schemes his way in with his small group of followers, disrupting the peace and bestowing wealth on those who do his bidding. Following the pattern already established in this vision, this northern ruler takes a large army up against the massive military of the king of the south and wins. He wins not because of might but because the southern king is undermined from within. Deception reigns in this storyline, for even when the two kings meet to share a meal, nothing they say to the other can be trusted.

The northern ruler returns home with his wealth, only to not be satisfied enough with these spoils to deter him from attacking the south twice more—the first being interrupted by the "Ships of Kittim"* and the latter resulting in his overwhelming many nations like a furious flood. In between, he battles against God and God's holy people.

This northern ruler reminds us of the fourth beast, who was different from the first three in chapter 7. "Unique" was how it was described. From it we saw a little horn emerge who grew to the south, to the east, and to the holy land. We imagined this horn trampling the holy place and see his animosity being expressed against God and God's people. And just as this horn became associated with Antiochus IV Epiphanes, this master of intrigue in chapter 11 becomes associated with Antiochus IV as well. These exploits described

---

* Kitam is listed as a descendant of Noah's son Japheth in Genesis 10:4. *The New Interpreter's Study Bible* associates Japheth's descendants with modern-day Turkey, Greece, and Cyprus. (Theodore Hiebert, Study notes on Genesis 10:2–5, in *The New Interpreter's Study Bible, New Revised Standard Version with Apocrypha*. (Nashville, TN: Abingdon Press, 2003), 23.) 1 Maccabees 1:1 claims that Alexander the Great came from Kittim (*Apocrypha*).

in this vision, with the exception of the last battle,[21] align with his Syrian military's acts of aggression against Egypt[22] in 170 and 168 BC.[23] And like the ruler in Daniel 11:30 being interrupted by ships from the west,[24] Antiochus was interrupted by Roman ships commanded by Gaius Popillius Laenas.[25] Likewise, the co-regent of Egypt, Ptolemy VI,[26] was undermined from within his household.

TIME OF REFLECTION

Go Deeper: 2 Maccabees 3

2 Maccabees 3 shares a powerful story about the intervention of God when a northern king sends a man named Heliodorus to claim for the king the money deposited by widows and orphans for safekeeping in the Temple treasury. The priest Onias and the people gather to pray and plead with God for protection. God responds by sending a vision of a horse with a rider clad in armor and gold who tramples Heliodorus and causes him true physical harm. As Heliodorus lies dying, Onias intercedes on his behalf and God heals him. As a result, Heliodorus becomes a believer and returns to the northern king empty-handed, except with a story of Divine safekeeping and deliverance. This story has become associated with the short-lived ruler of Daniel 11:20. And the righteous priest Onias III has become associated with the covenant leader of verse 22. How does hearing this story remind you that God is involved in the affairs of Daniel 11?

What did you learn about the character traits and the habits of the ruler introduced in verse 21?

Since there is incomplete fulfillment of the prophecies about this northern ruler, some say that this vision describes the anti-Christ who is yet to come. If this is the case, what are some context cues that people should be watching for in order to identify this anti-Christ figure?

COVENANT PEOPLE

Therefore *it is* of faith that *it might be* according to grace, so that the promise might be sure to all the seed, not only to those who are of the law but also to those who are of the faith of Abraham, who is the father of us all" (Romans 4:16 New King James Version). When we read of covenant people, we are reminded of the covenant God made with the people of Israel, through Abraham and later Moses, to be their God. We are also reminded of the New Covenant testified to in the New Testament, in which Jesus invites all those who are of the faith of Abraham to follow Him, to be God's people, and to be One.

When John the Baptist preached "Repent," he was calling people to turn from their sins and return to an active faith (Matthew 3). His audience at the time was the people of Israel, but his words have been heard through the generations since and have touched people of all ethnicities. We all have slipped and fallen short in reference to God's glory (Rom. 3:23). Even the apostle Peter denied knowing Jesus, the Son of God, just hours before His crucifixion! (John 18:17). Yet, after the resurrection, Jesus restored Peter by commissioning him with the instruction, "Tend my lambs" (John 21:15).

Zechariah prophesied a day when the people of Jerusalem would mourn over the crucifixion of God's son (Zechariah 12:10), a day in which idols would be cut off (Zech. 13:1–2). He also spoke of a time in which God's people would be cleansed and refined. Today's reading picks up with an emphasis on "covenant," "appointed time," and action taken. It calls out a warning to the covenant people that a time will come when people will abandon the holy covenant, but those who know God will be strong and take an active faith. Some will be murdered as a result. Others will stumble in their faith but will be refined in the process, which will prepare them to be "holy" when it is most needed: in the end.

The northern king's attacks against the covenant people will come in two waves. The first we read about in verses 22 and 28. The second is when his anger previously directed toward the south will be thwarted by the ships and redirected as rage against God's holy covenant. We start reading about this in verses 29 and 30.

As Daniel takes in this vision of atrocities against people like himself, those with wisdom, insight, and understanding who are committed to God and the covenant, one can only begin to imagine what must have been going through his mind. He has been told that this vision shows what will happen to his people in the last days (Daniel 10:14). But he is reassured throughout that "many will be purified, cleansed, and refined" and that "those who have insight will understand" (Dan. 12:10), and those with insight will "give understanding to many" (Dan. 11:33).

TIME OF REFLECTION

Go Deeper: Luke 22:54–62; John 21:15–17

The murder of people of the Jewish faith by Antiochus IV Epiphanes was only the beginning. In 202 AD, Roman emperor Septimius Severus declared that all converts to Judaism and Christianity and their teachers would be killed.[27] Later in the third century, Roman emperor Decius decided that a greater harm to Christianity than martyrdom would be getting these people of faith to turn against their own beliefs. So, Decius required everyone in the empire to sacrifice to the ancient Roman gods and burn incense before a statue of himself. Once this was done, all residents would receive a certificate testifying they did so. If they didn't receive this certificate, they would be considered outlaws and at risk of being tortured and persecuted further.[28] Within the church there became "confessors" who received torture in place of a certificate, those of privilege who cheated the system by purchasing certificates, and those who "lapsed" in some way, such as by burning incense or making the sacrifice, in order to receive a certificate.[29] After the end of this time of persecution, debate arose in the church about whether and how non-confessors could continue to be part of the Christian body. How do you think Daniel would weigh in on this debate based on his life experiences and the visions he received?

What do you think Daniel would have done had he been living under the rule of Antiochus IV Epiphanes, Septimius Severus, or Decius?

What does it mean to be a covenant people? Who are the covenant people?

THE ABOMINABLE SIGN

READ DANIEL 9:27, 11:31, 12:11–12

When I first read the description of the atrocities committed against the Temple in Jerusalem and the people of Judah during the reign of Antiochus IV Epiphanes, as recorded in 1 and 2 Maccabees, I was dumbfounded. How could I never have heard of these before? New mothers shamefully paraded and murdered for circumcising their infants; immoral sexual acts performed within sacred spaces; kosher-keeping people of faith forced to eat the non-kosher flesh of pigs; the sacred alter covered with sacrifices forbidden in Hebrew law; the Jerusalem Temple renamed after the name of the Greek god Zeus; and the people turned away from God's law and forbidden the practice of their holidays (1 Maccabees 1, 2 Maccabees 6). What disgusting affronts against God and God's people! I could no longer think of the words "abomination of desolation" as something that would only be offensive to God and the faithful. Antiochus fulfilled the words in dreadful ways. Yet, I also became concerned about a potential future time when the acts associated with these contaminating words would no longer be considered offensive to the common person. I wondered if Daniel really understood what he was writing about when he recorded the words "abomination of desolation" three times in this book. In his vision, did he see what this meant?

In Daniel 9:27, we read of a ruler who will end sacrifice and offering and will set up an "abomination of desolation" on the "wing of the temple," which will sustain until "the decreed destruction is poured out on the desolator."[30] Daniel 11:31 confirms these words, and Daniel 12:11 links these words with the vision of Daniel 8 by naming a specific number of days that will come to pass, 1,290, and then 45 days later, 1,335. If we reflect on Daniel 8:11–14, we also see the theme of an expected rebellion. This will all take place during the middle of the "week" of Daniel 9:27.

Jesus was familiar with these texts from Daniel. The memory of both the suffering under Antiochus and the messianic response in the Maccabean revolt were still relatively fresh in the memories of his people. Yet, Jesus still spoke of the prophecy of Daniel as a prophecy that remained to be fulfilled. He expected a time of great persecution still to come. When His disciples showed surprising insight by asking Him what would be the sign of His coming and when the end times would occur, Jesus gave a lengthy answer that is recorded in Matthew 24 and worth a read. He warned that when a person sees ...

> "the abomination of desolation, spoken by the prophet Daniel, standing in the holy place ... then those in Judea must flee to the mountains ... Woe to pregnant women and nursing mothers in those days! For at that time there will be great distress, the kind that hasn't taken place from the beginning of the world until now and never will again. ..." (Matthew 24:15–21)

He continues by explaining that in the future, many will claim to have come in his name, claiming to be the Messiah, and they are not to be believed (Matt. 24:4–5):

> "For as the lightning comes from the east and flashes as far as the west, so will be the coming of the Son of Man ... the sun will be darkened, and the moon will not shed its light; the stars will fall from the sky, and the powers of the heavens will be shaken. Then the sign of the Son of Man will appear in the sky, and then all the peoples of the earth will mourn; and they will see the Son of Man coming on the clouds of heaven with power and great glory." (Matt. 24:27, 29b–30)

Jesus associated the abomination of desolation with end-times events. The worst assault ever experienced by humanity is followed by the greatest victory ever witnessed in the arrival of the Son of Man in clouds of glory.

The angels testified to this same message. For after Jesus's resurrection and immediately following His ascension into the clouds, the messengers revealed that "This same Jesus, who has been taken from you into heaven, will come in the same way that you have seen him going into heaven" (Acts 1:9–11).

Yet, as prophetic fulfillment goes, there have been cycles of history that have seemed to fulfill Daniel's prophecy. Jerome pointed out that Pilate had put an image of Caesar in the Temple, and during Jerome's time, a statue of Hadrian stood in the Holy of Holies.[31] And history has recorded the Roman conquest of Jerusalem, the destruction of the Temple by Titus in 70 AD, and the persecution of that same era. But we have yet to see the return of The Christ.

We are to keep watch. The abomination of desolation is to be a sign for us, a warning to seek shelter, and a reminder to hold onto hope and look up because the Son of Man is on his way!

TIME OF REFLECTION

Go Deeper: Matthew 23:37–26:2

Re-read the first paragraph of this devotional. How do you see desolations like the ones listed taking place in your culture? Where do you see blatant forms of resistance against monotheistic religion? How about subtle forms? How do you stand up against such atrocities?

How does knowing that the days of trouble are numbered help a person get through those days?

Read Matthew 23:37 to 26:2. What do you want to remember about what you read?

CHRIST VERSUS ANTI-CHRIST

READ DANIEL 11:36–39

The ultimate act of betrayal is a person claiming to be the one true God, gaining our worship, and then not being that god. As theologians have given the label "anti-Christ" to this person who will rule in end times, there is a recognition that this person will be the antithesis of who Jesus is, while still claiming something similar. While Jesus is Truth, this anti-Christ is all about deception. While Jesus is good, the anti-Christ is not. While Jesus was humble and "… being in very nature God, did not consider equality with God something to be used to his own advantage …" (Philippians 2:6 NIV), this anti-Christ will claim to be greater than God and use the claim of this power to his own advantage and the advantage of the small crew who expresses allegiance to him. While Jesus was not a man of wealth, this anti-Christ figure will be focused on attaining material fortune. This anti-Christ figure will be successful because God will choose not to interfere "until the time of wrath is completed."[32]

This northern king of the last part of Daniel 11 not only claims superiority over the God of Israel but also over any gods that have been worshipped by any religious group. That is until his allegiance is expressed toward a god of fortresses. It seems significant that this prophecy identifies this god of fortresses as one that is both unknown to the northern king's ancestors and foreign. Who or what is this fortress god? And what power or activity does it represent? Or is this idea of "god" more representative of any object one glorifies, such that it could be this ruler's obsession with power, control, or material wealth rather than the uplifting of a false deity?

TIME OF REFLECTION

Go Deeper: John 8; Philippians 2:5–11

The most dangerous claim a person could make is the claim that he or she is the God of gods and it not be true. This person either doesn't believe that the Ultimate Deity exists or, if they do believe, they don't think this God will respond negatively to them making such a false claim.

Jesus made such a claim. In a lengthy conversation with His Jewish counterparts about His own identity, Jesus said to them, "Truly, truly, I say to you, before Abraham was born, I am" (John 8:58 NASB). His listeners understood this to be a claim of deity (see Exodus 3) as indicated by them immediately picking up rocks to stone him for the crime of blasphemy. The contrast between the northern king of Daniel 11, who claims to be the God of gods, and the man Jesus of the New Testament is striking! As we saw in Antiochus Epiphanes, his power and influence eventually passed as he became just a name in the history books. In contrast, the name of Jesus still leads to people bowing the knee and lifting up songs of thanksgiving and praise (Phil. 2:10–11).

The question for today is likely the most important question you'll ever be asked, and it has two parts. Is Jesus who He claimed to be? (see John 8). If so, are you willing to place your trust in Him?

LIKE A FLOOD!

One of the most recognized stories of the Bible is the story of Noah and the flood. We love to tell this story to children because it includes a boat, animals, and a rainbow, which all seem very child-friendly and reassuring that God isn't going to flood the earth again. Yet, we often skim over the reason for this great flood in the first place: God was grieved by the creation and the way that humanity was inclined toward evil, so God decided it was time to start over, to wipe the slate clean (Genesis 6–9). Once again, we look to the words of Jesus in Matthew 24:

> "As the days of Noah were, so the coming of the Son of Man will be. For in those days before the flood they were eating and drinking, marrying and giving in marriage, until the day Noah boarded the ark. They didn't know until the flood came and swept them all away. This is the way the coming of the Son of Man will be." (Matthew 24:37–39)

As in the days of Noah, when God chose to preserve a remnant of all of creation in an ark, so in the days of Christ's coming a remnant will be preserved. Jesus explains in Matthew 25:

> "When the Son of Man comes in his glory, and all the angels with him, then he will sit on his glorious throne. All the nations will be gathered before him, and he will separate them one from another, just as a shepherd separates the sheep from the goats. He will put the sheep on his right and the goats on the left. Then the King will say to those on his right, 'Come, you who are blessed by my father, inherit the Kingdom prepared for you from the foundation of the world.'" (Matt. 25:31–34)

In Daniel 9:26, we read that "The end will come with a flood, and until the end there will be war; desolations are decreed."[33] As we read further in Daniel, we see this use of the word "flood" to describe military aggression. The sons of a king "will advance, sweeping through like a flood."[34] Later, the king of the north will "sweep through them like a flood."[35]

TIME OF REFLECTION

Go Deeper: Genesis 6:5–22; Matthew 25:31–46

We are living in a time when there is an unprecedented quantity of natural disasters taking place globally.* Because of this, there is an ongoing conversation about climate change and a sense that the earth is falling apart. In Romans 8:18–21, we read:

> "I consider that our present sufferings are not worth comparing with the glory that will be revealed in us. For the creation waits in eager expectation for the children of God to be revealed. For the creation was subjected to frustration, not by its own choice, but by the will of the one who subjected it, in hope that the creation itself will be liberated from its bondage to decay and brought into the freedom and glory of the children of God." (NIV)

There is a hope underlying the book of Daniel of a time in which God's Messiah would come and restore Creation. A hope of God establishing God's good and life-full Kingdom here on earth. In the midst of reading about the destruction of war in the book of Daniel and considering natural disasters taking place across the globe today, how do the visions of Daniel also give us hope?

---

* For proof of this, watch the videos provided by The Two Preachers on YouTube. https://www.youtube.com/c/TheTwoPreachers.

How will the end times be experienced "like a flood"?

What is the warning for us in this story?

How does the biblical symbolism of the "rainbow" still speak to us today? (See Gen. 8:15–9:17.)

THE NORTH'S
FINAL BATTLES

─────────── READ DANIEL 11:40–45 ───────────

This last part of the prophecy has not yet been tied to any historical events. It is agreed that it is prophecy yet to be fulfilled. It begins, "At the time of the end ..."[36] and we read of the southern king engaging the northern in battle. We then read of the advancement of the northern king and of the great quantity of territory and wealth he amasses. This includes Egypt, which has played a dominant role throughout the Bible; Libya, a desert land in northern Africa just west of Egypt; and Cush, a land associated since Genesis with powerful warriors, as these are the descendants of Noah's son Ham, including Nimrod. (These lands include Babylon, Assyria, and Nineveh [Genesis 10:8–12], which are now associated with Sudan, Ethiopia, and sometimes the Arabian Peninsula.) Both ancient Jerome[37] and Theodoret of Cyr[38] saw Egypt, Libya, and Cush as the three horns of Daniel chapter 7.

We read that this northern king will even "invade the beautiful land,"* but the Edomites, Moabites, and Ammonites will escape. The history of these three people groups goes all the way back to Genesis. According to Genesis 19:36–38, the Moabites and Ammonites are the descendants of Abraham's brother Lot and Lot's two daughters who escaped Sodom with him. The Edomites are the children of Abraham's grandson Esau and Esau's Canaanite wives, including Ishmael's daughter (Gen. 36:1–9). These three people groups were often recognized as the enemies of Israel in the Old Testament: the Edomites living south of the Dead Sea, the Moabites directly east of the Dead Sea, and the Ammonites east of the Jordan River, the collective area known as Jordan today.

Unsurprisingly, when this northern king feels threatened from the north and the east, he will respond to his fear with destructive fury. Eventually,

─────────────────────────────

* Israel or the Holy Land.

though, he will settle down between the Mediterranean Sea and the "holy mountain," which Daniel defined in Daniel 9:16 as Jerusalem. Of course, after all of that tyrannical behavior, when this king finds himself in need, no one will be there to help him survive.

An alternative interpretation is that these final verses of chapter 11 are not about a king of the north but about a king who will be threatened by both a king of the south and a king of the north. This interpretation does not seem to see continuity between verses 35 and 36 but a break with an introduction of a new ruler.

TIME OF REFLECTION

Go Deeper: Genesis 10:8–12, 19:36–38, 36:1–9

What have you heard about a final battle before the return of Christ? Do you think this correlates with what you have read here in Daniel? What other books of the Bible may inform your understanding of the final events prior to Christ's return?

Looking back over all of chapter 11, do you find any correlation between other historical or contemporary events and the events of this chapter?

ACTION

Look back at the timeline you've created for previous chapters of Daniel. How would you extend your timeline with what you have learned from this past chapter? Create a timeline based on what you have learned from this chapter.

DANIEL 12

(The final chapter.)

SLEEP AND AWAKE!

THE GREAT ESCAPE

---- READ DANIEL 12:1–3 ----

We are to expect a "great tribulation" (Matthew 24:21), a time that is to come that is unlike anything we've seen before. But we must remember that our God is a god who delivers his people, delivering them from the enemy (Psalm 18:17), from temptations and sin (1 Corinthians 10:13; 2 Timothy 4:18), and even from death itself (Ps. 116:8, 2 Corinthians 1:9–10). Those saints who come out of this great tribulation, who have remained faithful to God through Christ, will then find themselves before God's throne. Here they will experience a beautiful intimacy with God as the One who "dwell[s] among them"[1] (Revelation 7:9–17).

In this passage from Daniel, we read about a book that contains the names of those who will be delivered. Later, the prophet Malachi writes of a "book of remembrance" being put together "for those who feared the LORD and had high regard for his name" (Malachi 3:16). God will show compassion toward those whose names are written in this book (Mal. 3:17).

What else does the Bible say about this book and those whose names are contained within it? In Luke 10, we learn that Jesus sent out seventy people to be a witness and prepare the spiritual ground for where he was about to go so that the spiritual harvest could be great. When they returned, he told them to rejoice "because your names are written in heaven" (Luke 10:20b NKJV). Paul and Timothy, in their letter to the Philippians, recognize their fellow ministers, Euodia, Syntyche, and Clement, as having their names written in the book of life (Philippians 4:2–3). The book of Revelation (3:5, 13:8, 17:8, 20:12, 21:27, and 22:19) tells us there is a book of life belonging to the Lamb in which the saints' names are inscribed and from which Jesus will advocate. According to Revelation 20, the saints from the first resurrection will rule with Christ on earth for a thousand years and then Satan will be fully defeated. After this, the remaining of the dead will rise to life for judgment. Then books of judgment will be opened that record the works of the dead. Additionally, the book of life will be opened, and those whose names are written in it will be spared "the lake of fire" (Rev. 20:15 NKJV). They will be witness to the appearance of a new heaven and the new earth. They will be able to bask in the glory of God and the beauty of the New Jerusalem with its river of life flowing from the throne of God. Then God and the saints will rule forevermore (Rev. 21–22).

TIME OF REFLECTION

Go Deeper: Psalm 116; Matthew 24:21–32

In Acts 14:22, we read of Paul and his companions encouraging the people of faith in Lystra, Iconium, and Antioch, saying, "We must through many tribulations enter the kingdom of God" (NKJV). And in Romans 5:3b–5, we are encouraged that "tribulation produces perseverance; and perseverance, character; and character, hope" (NKJV). Although we haven't lived through the great tribulation, on a personal level, most of us have lived through minor tribulations. What has helped you to keep the faith during those times?

How has your faith been strengthened by times of tribulation?

INCREASE IN KNOWLEDGE

──────────────── READ DANIEL 12:4 ────────────────

W hen I was a child, the World Wide Web, more commonly known as the internet, was new. My first-grade class had the privilege of being part of an educational experiment where we would write brief letters and send them as messages through our computer to a classmate's father in New York, and he would write back to us. This was considered quite innovative at the time. By fourth grade, the internet became something we could access in our homes by connecting our desktop computers to a modem that would then connect through our landline phones to the web. Like the fear that surrounded wiring homes with electricity in prior generations, there was fear about allowing this great new world into the home through the internet. Some said that to open your house in this way was to let the devil in. Little did we know.

As I write this, the internet has become a part of daily life. We use it to access news stories, to talk to our friends, to informally debate cultural values, to inform our worldview, and even to make medical decisions. While many expected it to bring us closer together, which it has globally, it has also exaggerated our differences. Knowing right from wrong, what is true from falsehoods, and what is real and what is produced have become unclear to many. Instead of our going to God for wisdom, people now browse the internet for answers to their questions. Our trust has been transferred from relying on the Divine One to relying on the collective conscious. And the gaining of this new knowledge has made ethical questions all the more complicated.*

In the book of Genesis, we read the story of beginnings, the most famous of stories being either the story of creation or the story of the great flood. In Genesis 1:29–30, we are told that on the sixth day, God created vegetation,

───

* For example, human knowledge of genetics and the early development of the human in the womb, as well as medical advancements to sustain the life of a person who would have otherwise died, have created new ethical dilemmas that previous generations never encountered.

including trees that bear fruit that would be our food. Then in the second part of Genesis 2:9, we learn that in this beautiful garden that God was creating, God placed the tree of life and the tree of the knowledge of good and evil. The fruit of the tree of life granted the inhabitants of earth access to eternal life (Genesis 3:22). We were welcomed to eat of this tree and almost all others. There was one tree whose fruit we weren't to eat, and that was the tree of the knowledge of good and evil (Gen. 2:16–17). The presence of this tree and this single rule gave humanity the opportunity to choose either faith-filled submission and obedience to God or self-reliant disobedience to God. What did the first humans do? They chose to eat from the single forbidden tree.* This resulted in an immediate loss of innocence, a first experience of shame and guilt, and the consequence that has become known as the "curse." Life became more difficult, and the people were no longer allowed access to the tree of life.

At the end of Daniel, as humanity prepares for the opportunity again to access the Garden of Eden and the tree of life, we read that Daniel is to keep secret the revelation he has received and to seal this book until end times. He is told that "Many will roam about, and knowledge will increase."[2]

We have been given access to the mind of God through reflection upon God's creation, the written word of the Bible, the life and work of Jesus Christ, and the gift of the Holy Spirit living within us and the Church. In contrast to the internet, these sources of knowledge are transformative and life-giving. The Pentecost event, fifty days after the ascension of Christ, represents a paradigm-shifting moment that changed the world (Acts 2). By allowing every human being who is willing to accept Christ and His message to be filled with God's Spirit and to have their mind renewed by this intimate connection with God, human knowledge was transformed and the mysteries of God were revealed. In the New Testament, a contrast is made between the wisdom of the world and God's wisdom (1 Corinthians 3:18–23). God's wisdom

---

† Interestingly, in contemporary US depictions of this story, an apple is frequently used to symbolize the fruit of the tree of knowledge of good and evil. One famous technology company that has had great influence in the development of computers and the internet uses in its branding the symbol of an apple with a bite removed from it. Although this is likely unintentional, could this coincidence have spiritual significance?

is revealed in the cross and in the Spirit, which are perceived by the flesh to be foolishness (1 Cor. 1:23–24, 2:10–12). But, oh, what great wisdom this is!

TIME OF REFLECTION

Go Deeper: 1 Corinthians 1–2; Revelation 22

Take a moment to reflect upon these verses:

> "The fear of the LORD is the beginning of wisdom,
>   and the knowledge of the Holy One is understanding.
> For by me your days will be many,
>   and years will be added to your life." (Proverbs 9:10–11)

> "It is because of him that you are in Christ Jesus, who has
>   become for us wisdom from God—that is, our righteousness,
>   holiness and redemption." (1 Cor. 1:30)

How does Scripture define "wisdom"?

How have you witnessed an "increase in knowledge" during your lifetime? Would you consider this a sign of the end times? Why or why not?

How does the knowledge gained from online technologies contrast with the knowledge gained from God? Which do you go to first for help—God or the internet?

The earth was created perfectly, but then humans chose to disobey God, and we have continued to do so for generations. The result is that the earth is now subject to decay. Yet, Scripture promises its restoration as the children of God are revealed. Romans 8 speaks of this and instructs us to live by the Spirit and not by the flesh. How is the condition of creation linked with the actions of humans?

FINAL THINGS

———— READ DANIEL 12:5–7, 10–13; 2 PETER 3:8–13 ————

"Teach us to number our days carefully so that we may develop wisdom in our hearts" (Psalm 90:12). As Daniel comes to the end of this vision, he is reminded that his own life is nearing its end. He will die before the events of the vision come to pass, but his sleep won't be forever, as he will rise to receive an inheritance at the end of days. The being above the waters raises his hands toward heaven and recognizes the One who lives eternally. We are reminded that death doesn't get the final say. There is an eternal God! There is resurrection!

Two of Jesus's female friends, Martha and Mary, take center stage in more than one New Testament story. When their brother Lazarus dies, Martha confronts Jesus about His not coming earlier to prevent Lazarus's death. She then begs Him to restore her brother to life. Jesus responds by saying, "Your brother will rise again" (John 11:23). Martha gives a faith-filled response, "I know that he will rise again in the resurrection of the last day" (John 11:24). To which Jesus makes the bold claim, "I am the resurrection and the life. The one who believes in me, even if he dies, will live. Everyone who lives and believes in me will never die. Do you believe this?" (John 11:25–26).

Throughout the letters of the New Testament, we read about this holy expectation of resurrection to life. Included in these letters are directions about how we are to live in the meantime. For example, in 1 Thessalonians, we are reminded that we belong to the light and, as such, "Since we belong to the day, let us be self-controlled and put on the armor of faith and love, and a helmet of the hope of salvation" (1 Thessalonians 5:8).

Sometimes that day of resurrection seems a long time in coming. People keep talking about "end times." And the "end times" always seems both imminent and distant, as if Jesus could return tomorrow or we could be waiting a few more millennia. We ask, "How long?" We are reminded that God is not in a hurry for this day to arrive because God is good and merciful and cares for humanity. In 2 Peter 3:8–9, we read:

> "Dear friends, don't overlook this one fact: With the Lord one day is like a thousand years, and a thousand years like one day. The Lord does not delay his promise, as some understand delay, but is patient with you, not wanting any to perish but all to come to repentance."

I am reminded of the first church where I served as a youth pastor. A group of middle school students were interested in reading fictitious stories about the end of days. There had also been conversations among the adults about a movie that had been released that made similar references. I asked the senior pastor how he suggested dealing with conversations on these topics. He said, "Remind them that these stories are fictitious interpretations of the biblical text, but that we all will face a personal end of days, and for some of us that day will come sooner than for others."

Martha responded to Jesus, "Yes, Lord . . . I believe you are the Messiah, the Son of God, who comes into the world."[3] How do you respond when Jesus asks, "Do you believe this?"[4]

TIME OF REFLECTION

Go Deeper: 1 Thessalonians 4–5

Take time to reflect upon the life that Daniel lived. What have you learned about life and faith from Daniel's example?

Have you, like Daniel, committed yourself to absolute devotion to God?

What does it mean to "number your days"?

Are you ready to believe that Jesus is the resurrection, the life, the Messiah, and the Son of God?

SEALED UNTIL THE END

—————— READ DANIEL 12:8–9, 13; REVELATION 22:7–10 ——————

Throughout the book of Daniel, we read stories of visions and dreams in which the message is concealed in obscurity, only to be discovered by righteous Daniel as he seeks God in prayer and uses past prophecies and Scripture as a resource for understanding. Here in chapter 12, we are reminded that some are righteous and others are not. When the timing is right, God will reveal the meaning of visions to the righteous. They will be lifted up and enlightened, while others will be brought to shame (Daniel 12:2).

As we have interpreted Daniel, we have seen how both the recordkeeping and evolution of history have helped us gain a greater understanding of some of the mysteries shared within Daniel. We have learned about Antiochus IV Epiphanes, about the Syrian Wars, and wondered about how future events may fulfill Scripture in new ways. We have been given a holy expectation of a time in which the Son of God is revealed in a new way and the saints are given authority.

The New Testament encourages us as we are told that the mysteries of God are revealed through Christ Jesus, the Son (Ephesians 1:3–10 and Colossians 2:3) and through His Church (Eph. 3:4–12, Col. 1:15–27). We also receive a prophetic word about a scroll that is covered with seven seals that can only be opened by one who is worthy. And that one is found in the Lamb of God who is able to break the seals and reveal its contents—this same Lamb of God who took away the sins of the world. Revelation 5:9–10 reads:

> "And they sang a new song, saying,
>
> 'Worthy are You to take the book and to break its seals;
> for You were slain, and purchased for God with Your blood
> men from every tribe and tongue and people and nation.
> You have made them to be a kingdom and priests to our God;
> and they will reign upon the earth.'" (NASB)

Isn't it amazing to think that God would reveal to us mere humans his plans for us? We have this compilation of books from Genesis to Revelation that shows us who God is, who we are to be as God's people, and where the earthly timeline is going. Isn't this amazing! How can we not feel a sense of personal connectedness to a God who cares enough to let us know where we are going? My heart, my mind, my soul, and my body worship this God who calls me by name and invites me into the most wonderful story ever told! Will you worship God with me?

TIME OF REFLECTION

Go Deeper: Ephesians 1:1–14; Revelation 5

Multiple times in the Bible, we read of a mark or a seal being placed on God's faithful people to protect them. In Exodus 12, as the angel of death passed through the land, those who had the blood of a lamb on their doorframes were spared death. In Ezekiel 9:4, we read of an angel sealing the foreheads of those who grieved over the abominations of idolatry witnessed in the Temple, and in doing so spared their lives with the mark of a "tav," which looked like a cross.[5] In Revelation 9, we are told that when the fifth angel sounds the horn, only those who have the seal of God on their foreheads are guaranteed safety. In the Old Testament, a king would mark his official documents with a seal so the recipients would know that this letter was indeed from the king (Esther 8:8). How is the marking of the forehead of the faithful similar to a king placing a seal on a letter?

In Ephesians 1:13, we are told that those who hear the word of truth and believe this gospel of salvation are sealed with the Holy Spirit. Do you think you have been sealed with God's Spirit? Why or why not?

DANIEL, JOB, AND NOAH

READ EZEKIEL 14:12–23

Even if these three remain, only they themselves will be saved. Neither the righteousness of Job, Noah, or Daniel could save the people around them. Job was not even able to save his children. Neither can the righteousness of people like Mother Teresa, Rev. Dr. Martin Luther King Jr., or that saint you know in your community save those who witness their ministry. Even your own righteousness isn't enough to save yourself. The only person to have ever lived whose righteousness could save others is Jesus Christ.

The Bible clearly communicates that we are to clothe ourselves with Christ. Galatians 3:26–27, 29 proclaims:

> "So in Christ Jesus you are all children of God through faith, for all of you who were baptized into Christ have clothed yourselves with Christ ... If you belong to Christ, then you are Abraham's seed, and heirs according to the promise." (NIV)

When we are clothed with Christ, his righteousness becomes our own (1 Corinthians 1:30; 2 Corinthians 5:21).

Every good and perfect thing points to Jesus, who is the way, the truth, and the life (John 14:6). Daniel knew and believed in Christ. He saw his then-future coming and believed the message God had given him.

In Romans, we read,

> "For I am not ashamed of the gospel, because it is the power of God that brings salvation to everyone who believes; first to the Jew, then to the Gentile. For in the gospel the righteousness of God is revealed—a righteousness that is by faith from first to last, just as it is written: 'The righteous will live by faith.'" (Romans 1:16–17 NIV)

In Christ we find grace, forgiveness, and life. We find a path for life that is different than the path of life offered to us by the world. In the world, we are judged and condemned, but in Christ, we find a way forward. The truth in Christ liberates rather than imprisons. A relationship with Jesus Christ is transformative; it not only changes our own identity, but it also changes how we react to and interact with others. Those who are in Christ are empowered to share love, faith, and hope with the world. Of course, this change isn't always immediate; for some it may be, but for all who continue in faith, it is a journey of continual transformation that takes place as we worship God the Father, abide in Christ the Son, and allow God's Holy Spirit to be at work within us. We will fail. We will sin. We will hurt others and regret the harm we caused. But we can trust that God will work in transformative ways to bring about His eternal kingdom both within us and here on earth.

I have believed. And I trust God to carry me forward in that faith.

I pray that you might also be blessed with faith and be open to the work of God within you. Thank you for taking the time to draw near to God as you journeyed through the book of Daniel and *Resilient Faith*.

TIME OF REFLECTION

Go Deeper: Luke 24

How have you been open to the work of God in your life?

Do you believe that Jesus is the way, the truth, and the life?

Are you ready to take that step of faith and place your trust in the God of Israel who is made flesh in the Messiah Jesus? Will you receive God's gift to you of God's Holy Spirit?

ACTION

Make a list of seven things you have learned from the book of Daniel and *Resilient Faith* that you want to remember. Include in your list at least one belief you want to hold and one behavior you want to live.

1.

2.

3.

4.

5.

6.

7.

CONTEXT FOR WRITING THIS BOOK

I t has felt like the beginning of the last days now for some time. I began researching and writing this devotional when global society shut down in the spring of 2020 due to the COVID-19 pandemic. At that time, our country was in turmoil due to the drawing of political dichotomies. The closing down of normal life only exaggerated our individual and tribal distinctions.

The US president was Donald Trump, and he was a divisive character, whether intentionally or not. It was during his presidency that I began to hear references being made to how he was like King Nebuchadnezzar, as described in the book of Daniel. That, coupled with an increase in the severity and frequency of natural disasters, made it feel like the end times were upon us. I truly and wholeheartedly expected Jesus to show up that Easter!

I was also in a place in my life where I had read through the Bible in its entirety numerous times, and from the model of a friend, I wanted to dive into each book much deeper. So, I decided it was time for me to investigate more thoroughly the book of Daniel, which was often quoted with the expertise of the person sharing the information being taken for granted, and it was a book I knew little about. I wanted to see for myself what it actually said.

As I began to research and to write, I discovered that this book was a gem for understanding the Bible as a whole. It connects the Old and the New Testament, the beginning of time with the end, fulfilled prophecy with that which still lingers, and it embodies both submission to authorities and defiance against the oppressor. In my writing, in my attempts to understand this book and make that which seems inaccessible accessible to the common reader, I also discovered an opportunity to provide a form of discipleship. The storyline gave natural moments to help the reader understand biblical interpretation, Christian theology, and even at times the folk culture of US expressions of faith. I found myself not only writing a devotional commentary on Daniel but also a Bible study on the basics of faith that guide our spiritual growth.

The writing also became very personal at times. When researching the symbolism of trees, my two-year-old niece and I shared a precious moment when she recognized that the wood in the campfire was dead and it came from a living tree like the one next to our campsite. She expressed sadness for the tree and wanted us to stop burning its log. Just a few days later, I watched as a derecho bellowed its way through our community, destroying between 60–80 percent of the trees. I then experienced a crisis of faith, as the expected help was delayed and our local government appeared helpless while we went nearly two weeks without electricity. A year later, I found myself writing about "time, times, and half a time" on the morning of my fourtieth birthday.

As I came to the last vision of Daniel, I found myself pondering how Daniel went about understanding others' visions with fasting and prayer. Was I to do similarly in trying to understand this last quarter of the book? In my own devotional life, I came across the story of how Joseph told Pharaoh that when a dream was revealed twice, it meant that it had been decided by God and was about to be carried out (Genesis 41:32), something that was emphasized by the pastor who preached about vocational calling at my ordination. That next morning, I woke a little before 4 a.m. with a reminder about my own repetitive dreams and this idea rolling in my head about how the reordering of the chapters of Daniel was key to unveiling the mysteries of revelation contained in Daniel. This alone was reason enough for me to publish this devotional commentary.

As I struggled with how to approach the reference to the "prince" Michael dealing with the opposition of the "prince of Persia" in chapter 10, my country was grieving the loss of nineteen children, their two teachers, and the harm caused to their classmates in yet another school shooting. I finished writing the devotional and turned to see what was happening in the news, and I read a headline stating that there had just been an active shooting in a hospital. I asked God, "Is there something we are missing about the spiritual realm in how we are responding to shootings in the United States? Are we saying we are praying but actually not praying? Or maybe our prayers are ineffective because our lives are spiritually disconnected?" I added a note to my bathroom mirror to remind me to pray every day for the children of our nation.

This devotional turned out to be not only about the life of Daniel and the prophecies God directed toward him; it is also a book about the basics of faith and how to be resilient despite life's circumstances. Although this message seemed the most needed as we walked through and emerged from the global crisis of 2020, it is just as significant today. The linking of our former president with Nebuchadnezzar, whether appropriate or misplaced, was an invitation to go deeper into this book and to hear its message, to move past our political agendas or fears, and to let God's word speak on a deeper level to who we are and how we respond to a mighty God, to ultimately see God as our King—past, present, and in the future.

This is what I hope for you as a reader—that you have been challenged by this invitation to recognize God as supreme ruler and accept the invitation to worship God alone.

Author's Challenge to the Reader: Wouldn't it be great if people from several different churches within a community decided to do a Bible study together? Consider how you might play a role in bringing together followers of Christ from more than one church to study God's word together. Then initiate the small group and have fun!

BIBLIOGRAPHY

"'The Daniel 9:24-27 Project: The Framework for Messianic Chronology.' New Light on the Book of Daniel from the Dead Sea Scrolls. Ancient Manuscripts, Translations, and Texts." Associates for Biblical Research. Accessed December 7, 2021. https://biblearchaeology.org/research/the-daniel-9-24-27-project/4362-understanding-the-2-300-evenings-and-mornings-of-daniel-8-14.

Augustine, *Confessions*. Translated by Henry Chadwick. Oxford: Oxford University Press, 1991.

Augustine, "Letters." In *Fathers of the Church, A New Translation*. Translated by Wilfred Parsons and Robert B. Eno, 30: 76-77. Washington, D.C.: The Catholic University of America Press, 1951-1989.

Barker, Kenneth L. "Daniel." In *NASB Study Bible*, 1226-1248. Grand Rapids, MI: Zondervan Publishing House, 1999.

Barker, Kenneth L. "Ezekiel." In *NASB Study Bible*, 1156-1225. Grand Rapids, MI: Zondervan Publishing House, 1999.

Barker, Kenneth L. "Ptolemies and Seleucids." Chart. In *NASB Study Bible*, 1246–47. Grand Rapids, MI: Zondervan Publishing House, 1999.

Barry, John D. "Daniel." In *NKJV Faithlife Illustrated Study Bible*, 1387-1416. Grand Rapids, MI: Zondervan, 2018.

"Belshazzar." Online Etymology Dictionary. Accessed January 10, 2022. https://www.etymonline.com/word/Belshazzar.

"Berenice." *Encyclopædia Britannica*. Encyclopædia Britannica, Inc. Accessed March 19, 2022. https://www.britannica.com/biography/Berenice-daughter-of-Ptolemy-II.

Berkowitz, L. and K. Squiter, eds. *Thesaurus Linguae Graecae: Canon of Greek Authors and Works,* 2nd ed. Oxford: Oxford University Press, 1985-.

Berlin, Adele and Marc Zvi Brettler (adapted by). "Historical and Geographical Background to the Bible." In *Tanakh Translation, The Jewish Study Bible,* 2048-2062. New York, NY: Oxford University Press, 2004.

Cargill, Robert R. *The Cities That Built the Bible.* New York, NY: HarperCollins Publishers, 2016.

Chrysostom, John. *On the Priesthood, Ascetic Treatises, Select Homilies and Letters, Homilies on the Statues.* Edited by Philip Schaff. Oxford Translation revised by W.R.W. Stephens. 14 vols. Series 1. Peabody, MA: Hendrickson, 1994.

"The Didache." St. Gemma Web Productions Inc. 2005-2011. Accessed October 6, 2022. http://www.thedidache.com/.

Fernando, Ajith, Wayne Grudem, and J.I. Packer, et al., eds. "Daniel." In *Global Study Bible*, 1145-1173. Wheaton, IL: Crossway, 2012.

Gonzalez, Justo L. *The Story of Christianity: Volume I: The Early Church to the Dawn of the Reformation.* San Francisco, CA: HarperSanFrancisco, 1984.

Hasel, Gerhard. "New Light on the Book of Daniel from the Dead Sea Scrolls." Ancient Texts: Book of Daniel from Dead Sea Scrolls - Associates for Biblical Research, July 12, 2012. https://biblearchaeology.org/research/topics/ancient-manuscripts/3193-new-light-on-the-book-of-daniel-from-the-dead-sea-scroll.

"H2532 – Ḥemdâ – Strong's Hebrew Lexicon (KJV)." Blue Letter Bible. Accessed October 6, 2022. https://www.blueletterbible.org/lexicon/h2532/kjv/wlc/0-1/.

Henze, Matthias. Study notes on "Daniel." In *The New Interpreter's Study Bible, New Revised Standard Version with Apocrypha,* edited by Walter J. Harrelson, 1551-1593. Nashville, TN: Abingdon Press, 2003.

Hiebert, Theodore. Study notes on "Genesis." In *The New Interpreter's Study Bible, New Revised Standard Version with Apocrypha,* edited by Walter J. Harrelson, 1-84. Nashville, TN: Abingdon Press, 2003.

Hippolytus, "Scholia on Daniel." In *Hippolytus, Cyprian, Caius, Novatian.* Edited by A. Roberts and J. Donaldson. Translated by S.D.F. Salmond, 185-191. 10 vols. 1885-1887. Reprint, Peabody, MA.: Hendrickson, 1994.

Jagran Prakashan Limited (JPL). "National Emblem of Different Countries." General Knowledge List. General Knowledge. Jagran Josh. Last modified on May 14, 2014. Accessed June 4, 2021. http://www.jagranjosh.com/general-knowledge/national-emblem-of-different-countries-1399878043-1.

Jeffrey, Grant R., ed. "Daniel." In *NIV Prophecy Marked Reference Study Bible,* 959-996. Grand Rapids, MI: Zondervan Publishing House, 1998.

Jeremiah, David. *The Handwriting on the Wall: Secrets from the Prophecies of Daniel.* Dallas: Word Publishing, 1992.

LaCocque, André. "Daniel." In *Global Bible Commentary*, edited by Daniel Patte, 253-261. Nashville, TN: Abingdon Press, 2004.

Leander of Seville, "The Training of Nuns." *Iberian Fathers: Martin of Braga, Paschasius of Dumium, Leander of Seville.* Translated by Claude W. Barlow, 183-228. Washington, DC: Catholic University of America Press, 1969.

Loades, David. "The Early Reception." In *The Acts and Monuments Online* (essay). 2011. Accessed on January 22, 2022. https://www.johnfoxe.org/index_realm_more_goto-type_modern_type_essay_book_essay7.html.

Migne, J.P., ed. *Patrologie cursus completus.* Series Graeca. 166 vols. Paris: Migne, 1857-1886.

New York City Department of Planning. "GOAT: Geographic Online Address Translator." GeoSport. Accessed December 14, 2021. http://a030-goat.nyc.gov/goat/.

Ramsey, Russ, John Greco, and Trevin Wax. "The Time Between the Testaments." In *He Reads Truth Bible*, edited by Raechel Myers and Amanda Bible Williams, 1668–69. Nashville, TN: Holman Bible Publishers, 2019.

Ramsey, Russ, John Greco, and Trevin Wax. "Timeline: Nehemiah and the Babylonian Captivity." In *He Reads Truth Bible*, edited by Raechel Myers and Amanda Bible Williams, 764-765. Nashville, TN: Holman Bible Publishers, 2019.

Roberts, A. and J. Donaldson, eds. *Ante-Nicene Fathers.* 10 vols. Buffalo, NY: Christian Literature, 1885-86. Reprint, Grand Rapids, MI: Eerdmans, 1951-1956. Reprint, Peabody, MA: Hendrickson, 1994.

Schaff, Phillip et al., eds. *A Select Library of the Nicene and Post-Nicene Fathers of the Christian Church.* 2 series (14 vols. each). Buffalo, NY: Christian Literature, 1887-1894. Reprint, Grand Rapids, MI: Eerdmans, 1952-1956. Reprint, Peabody, MA: Hendrickson, 1994.

Simonetti, Manilo, ed. *Ancient Christian Commentary: Matthew 14-28.* Downers Grove, IL: InterVarsity Press, 2002.

Stevenson, Kenneth, and Michael Glerup, eds. *Ancient Christian Commentary; Ezekiel, Daniel*. Downers Grove, IL: InterVarsity Press, 2008.

Sweeney, Marvin A., "Daniel." In *Tanakh Translation, The Jewish Study Bible,* 1652. New York, NY: Oxford University Press, 2004.

Sweeney, Marvin A., "Ezekiel." In *Tanakh Translation, The Jewish Study Bible,* 1042-1138. New York, NY: Oxford University Press, 2004.

Tertullian, and Roberts, A. and Donaldson, J., eds. *Latin Christianity: Its Founder, Tertullian.* Translated by S. Thelwall. 10 vols. 1885-87. Reprint, Peabody, MA: Hendrickson, 1994.

Theodoret of Cyr, "Commentary on Daniel." In *Writings from the Greco-Roman World,* 7:123, Atlanta: Society of Biblical Literature, 2001-.

Theodoret of Cyr. *Commentary on Daniel.* Translated by Robert C. Hill. Boston: Brill, 2006.

Thompson, Frank Charles. "4434-Shusan or Susa." In *The Thompson Chain-Reference Bible, New King James Version*, 1245-1246. Indianapolis, IN: B.B. Kirkbride Bible Co., Inc., 1997.

Thompson, Frank Charles. *The Thompson Chain-Reference Bible, New King James Version.* Indianapolis, IN: B.B. Kirkbride Bible Co., Inc., 1997.

Walton, John H. and Craig S. Keener, eds. *NKJV Cultural Backgrounds Study Bible*. Grand Rapids, MI: Zondervan, 2017.

Walton, John H., ed. "Daniel." In *NKJV Cultural Backgrounds Study Bible,* 1461-1505. Grand Rapids, MI: Zondervan Publishing House, 2017.

Walvoord, John F. *Major Bible Prophecies: 37 Crucial Prophecies That Affect You Today.* Grand Rapids, MI: Zondervan Publishing House, 1991.

Walvoord, John F. *The Prophecy Knowledge Handbook.* Colorado Springs, CO: Victor Books, 1990.

Werner, R., ed. "Ptolemy I Soter." *Encyclopædia Britannica.* Encyclopædia Britannica, Inc. Accessed March 19, 2022. https://www.britannica.com/biography/Ptolemy-I-Soter.

Wikimedia Foundation. "Wikipedia: Anemoi." June 7, 2021. https://en.wikipedia.org/wiki/Anemoi.

Wikimedia Foundation. "Wikipedia: Chaldea." July 21, 2020. https://en.wikipedia.org/wiki/Chaldea.

Wikimedia Foundation. "Wikipedia: List of National Animals." June 4, 2021. http://en.wikipedia.org/wiki/List_of_national_animals.

Wikimedia Foundation. "Stacy Horn." November 23, 2021. https://en.wikipedia.org/wiki/Stacy_Horn.

Wikimedia Foundation. "Wikipedia: World tree." October 8, 2020. https://en.wikipedia.org/wiki/World_tree.

Williams, David S. "1 Maccabees." In *The New Interpreter's Study Bible, New Revised Standard Version with Apocrypha*, 1551-1593. Nashville, TN: Abingdon Press, 2003.

Wills, Lawrence M., "Daniel." In *Tanakh Translation, The Jewish Study Bible*, 1640-1665. New York, NY: Oxford University Press, 2004.

Worldhistory.us, "Cleopatra I Queen of Egypt." June 28, 2017. Accessed on April 20, 2022. https://worldhistory.us/ancient-history/ancient-egypt/cleopatra-i-queen-of-egypt.php.

Writings from the Greco-Roman World. Atlanta: Society of Biblical Literature, 2001-.

NOTES

DANIEL 1

1. Daniel 1:1 NIV.
2. Lawrence M. Wills, Annotations on Daniel 1:5, in *The Jewish Study Bible, Jewish Publication Society Tanakh Translation* (New York, NY: Oxford University Press, 2004), 1643.
3. Leander of Seville, "The Training of Nuns," in *Iberian Fathers: Martin of Braga, Paschasius of Dumium, Leander of Seville*, Translated by Claude W. Barlow (Washington, DC: Catholic University of America Press, 1969), 183-228. Quoted in *Fathers of the Church: A New Translation* (Washington, DC: Catholic University of America Press, 1947-), 62.

DANIEL 2

1. Daniel 2:15 NIV.
2. Daniel 2:22 NIV.
3. Grant R. Jeffrey, Daniel 2:37-40 footnote, in *NIV Prophecy Marked Reference Study Bible* (Grand Rapids, MI: Zondervan Publishing House, 1998), 967.
4. Jerome. *Commentary on Daniel*, 32. Translated by Gleason L. Archer, Jr. Grand Rapids, MI: Baker, 1958.

DANIEL 3

1. "Wikipedia: Chaldea," Wikimedia Foundation, accessed July 21, 2020, https://en.wikipedia.org/wiki/Chaldea.
2. Robert R. Cargill, *The Cities That Built the Bible* (New York, NY: HarperCollins Publishers, 2016), 81-82.
3. John Chrysostom, "Homilies Concerning the Statues." In *On the Priesthood, Ascetic Treatises, Select Homilies and Letters, Homilies on the Statues.* Oxford translation revised by W.R.W. Stephens. Series 1. Edited by Philip Schaff. 14 vols. 1886-1889 (Reprint, Peabody, MA: Hendrickson, 1994), 331-489.
4. Daniel 3:14 CSB.
5. Daniel 3:15 CSB.
6. Daniel 3:17 CSB.
7. Tertullian, "On Idolatry," in *Latin Christianity: Its Founder, Tertullian.* Translated by S. Thelwall. Edited by Alexander Roberts and James Donaldson. 10 vols. 1885-87 (Reprint, Peabody, MA: Hendrickson, 1994), 61-76.
8. Augustine, "Letters." In *Fathers of the Church, A New Translation.* Translated by Wilfred Parsons and Robert B. Eno (Washington, DC: The Catholic University of America Press, 1951-1989), 30:76-77.
9. Theodoret of Cyr, "Commentary on Daniel." Translated by Robert C. Hill (Boston: Brill, 2006). In *Writings from the Greco-Roman World* (Atlanta: Society of Biblical Literature, 2001-), 7:75-77.
10. Lawrence M. Wills, Annotations on Daniel 3:2, in *The Jewish Study Bible, Jewish Publication Society Tanakh Translation* (New York, NY: Oxford University Press, 2004), 1647.
11. Daniel 3:25 CSB.

DANIEL 4

1. Jerome. *Commentary on Daniel.* Translated by Gleason L. Archer, Jr. (Grand Rapids, MI: Baker, 1958), 51-52.

2. Kenneth Stevenson and Michael Glerup, eds., *"Ezekiel, Daniel,"* *Ancient Christian Commentary* (Downers Grove, IL: InterVarsity Press, 2008), 194-195.

3. Lawrence M. Wills, Annotations on Daniel 4:1-34, in *The Jewish Study Bible, Jewish Publication Society Tanakh Translation* (New York, NY: Oxford University Press, 2004), 1649.

4. "Wikipedia: World tree," Wikimedia Foundation, accessed October 8, 2020, https://en.wikipedia.org/wiki/World_tree.

5. Theodoret of Cyr, "Commentary on Daniel." Translated by Robert C. Hill (Boston: Brill, 2006). In *Writings from the Greco-Roman World* (Atlanta: Society of Biblical Literature, 2001-), 7:123.

6. Kenneth L. Baker, Daniel 4:16 footnote, in *nasb Study Bible* (Grand Rapids, MI: Zondervan Publishing House, 1999), 1233.

DANIEL 7

1. Grant R. Jeffrey, Daniel 7:1 footnote, in *niv Prophecy Marked Reference Study Bible* (Grand Rapids, MI: Zondervan Publishing House, 1998), 975.

2. Lawrence M. Wills, Daniel 7:1-28 footnote, in *Tanakh Translation, The Jewish Study Bible* (New York, NY: Oxford University Press, 2004), 1655.

3. "Wikipedia: Anemoi," Wikimedia Foundation, accessed June 7, 2021, last modified May 26, 2021, https://en.wikipedia.org/wiki/Anemoi.

4. Jerome. *Commentary on Daniel.* Translated by Gleason L. Archer, Jr. (Grand Rapids, MI: Baker, 1958), 71-72.

5. John Chrysostom, "Interpretatio in Danielem prophetam [Sp]. "In *Opera omnia.* Edited by J.P. Migne (Paris: Migne, 1859), 56:231, cols. 193-246. Quoted in *Thesaurus Linguae Graecae: Canon of Greek Authors and Works.* 2nd ed. Edited by L. Berkowitz and K. Squiter (Oxford: Oxford University Press, 1986), 2062-209.

6. Theodoret of Cyr, "Commentary on Daniel." Translated by Robert C. Hill (Boston: Brill, 2006). In *Writings from the Greco-Roman World* (Atlanta: Society of Biblical Literature, 2001-), 7:175-77.

7. St. Augustine, *Confessions,* trans. Henry Chadwick (Oxford: Oxford University Press, 1991), 296.

8. Daniel 7:12 csb.

9. Marvin A. Sweeney, Ezekiel 17:3-4 footnote, in *Tanakh Translation, The Jewish Study Bible* (New York, NY: Oxford University Press, 2004), 1071.

10. Marvin A. Sweeney, Ezekiel 17:7-8 footnote, in *Tanakh Translation, The Jewish Study Bible* (New York, NY: Oxford University Press, 2004), 1072.

11. Jerome. *Commentary on Daniel.* Translated by Gleason L. Archer Jr. (Grand Rapids, MI: Baker, 1958), 72-73.

12. "Wikipedia: List of National Animals," Wikimedia Foundation, accessed June 4, 2021, last modified May 27, 2021, https://en.wikipedia.org/wiki/List_of_national_animals.

13. "National Emblem of Different Countries," General Knowledge List, General Knowledge, Jagran Josh, Jagran Prakashan Limited (JPL), accessed June 4, 2021, last modified on May 14, 2014. http://www.jagranjosh.com/general-knowledge/national-emblem-of-different-countries-1399878043-1.

14. Kenneth Stevenson and Michael Glerup, eds., *Ancient Christian Commentary; Ezekiel, Daniel* (Downers Grove, IL: InterVarsity Press, 2008), 220.

15. André LaCocque, "Daniel," in *Global Bible Commentary*, ed. Daniel Patte (Nashville, TN: Abingdon Press, 2004), 256.

16. Theodoret of Cyr, "Commentary on Daniel." Translated by Robert C. Hill (Boston: Brill, 2006). In *Writings from the Greco-Roman World* (Atlanta: Society of Biblical Literature, 2001-), 7:179.

17. Hippolytus, "Scholia on Daniel." In *Hippolytus, Cyprian, Caius, Novatian.* Translated by S.D.F. Salmond. Edited by Alexander Roberts and James Donaldson. 10 vols. 1885-1887 (Reprint, Peabody, MA.: Hendrickson,

1994), 185-191. Quoted in A. Roberts and J. Donaldson, eds. *Ante-Nicene Fathers.* 10 vols. (Buffalo, NY: Christian Literature, 1885-86. Reprint, Grand Rapids, MI: Eerdmans, 1951-56. Reprint, Peabody, MA: Hendrickson, 1994), 5:189.

18. Theodoret of Cyr, "Commentary on Daniel." Translated by Robert C. Hill (Boston: Brill, 2006). In *Writings from the Greco-Roman World* (Atlanta: Society of Biblical Literature, 2001-), 7:179-81.

19. Grant R. Jeffrey, Daniel 7:5 footnote, in *NIV Prophecy Marked Reference Study Bible* (Grand Rapids, MI: Zondervan Publishing House, 1998), 976.

20. Grant R. Jeffrey, Daniel 7:5 footnote, in *NIV Prophecy Marked Reference Study Bible* (Grand Rapids, MI: Zondervan Publishing House, 1998), 975-976.

21. "Wikipedia: List of National Animals," Wikimedia Foundation, accessed June 4, 2021, last modified May 27, 2021, https://en.wikipedia.org/wiki/List_of_national_animals.

22. Theodoret of Cyr, "Commentary on Daniel." Translated by Robert C. Hill (Boston: Brill, 2006). In *Writings from the Greco-Roman World* (Atlanta: Society of Biblical Literature, 2001-), 7:181,183.

23. Lawrence M. Wills, Annotations on Daniel 7:4-8, in *The Jewish Study Bible, Jewish Publication Society Tanakh Translation* (New York, NY: Oxford University Press, 2004), 1656.

24. "National Emblem of Different Countries," General Knowledge List, General Knowledge, Jagran Josh, Jagran Prakashan Limited (JPL), accessed June 4, 2021, last modified on May 14, 2014. http://www.jagranjosh.com/general-knowledge/national-emblem-of-different-countries-1399878043-1.

25. "Wikipedia: List of National Animals," Wikimedia Foundation, accessed June 4, 2021, last modified May 27, 2021, https://en.wikipedia.org/wiki/List_of_national_animals.

26. André LaCocque, "Daniel," in *Global Bible Commentary*, ed. Daniel Patte (Nashville, TN: Abingdon Press, 2004), 254.

27. Daniel 7:23 NIV.

28. Daniel 2:40-43.

29. Lawrence M. Wills, Annotations on Daniel 7:4-8, in *The Jewish Study Bible, Jewish Publication Society Tanakh Translation* (New York, NY: Oxford University Press, 2004), 1656.

30. Jerome. *Commentary on Daniel.* Translated by Gleason L. Archer, Jr. (Grand Rapids, MI: Baker, 1958), 76-77.

31. Theodoret of Cyr, "Commentary on Daniel." Translated by Robert C. Hill (Boston: Brill, 2006). In *Writings from the Greco-Roman World* (Atlanta: Society of Biblical Literature, 2001-), 7:193-95.

32. Hippolytus, "Scholia on Daniel." In *Hippolytus, Cyprian, Caius, Novatian.* Translated by S.D.F. Salmond. Edited by Alexander Roberts and James Donaldson. 10 vols. 1885-1887 (Reprint, Peabody, MA.: Hendrickson, 1994), 185-191. Quoted in A. Roberts and J. Donaldson, eds. *Ante-Nicene Fathers.* 10 vols. (Buffalo, NY: Christian Literature, 1885-86. Reprint, Grand Rapids, MI: Eerdmans, 1951-56. Reprint, Peabody, MA: Hendrickson, 1994), 5:189.

33. Grant R. Jeffrey, Daniel 7:7-8 footnote, in *NIV Prophecy Marked Reference Study Bible* (Grand Rapids, MI: Zondervan Publishing House, 1998), 976.

34. Rev. 17:12-14.

35. André LaCocque, "Daniel," in *Global Bible Commentary*, ed. Daniel Patte (Nashville, TN: Abingdon Press, 2004), 255.

36. Raechel Myers and Amanda Bible Williams, eds. "The Time Between the Testaments," In *He Reads Truth Bible*, (Nashville, TN: Holman Bible Publishers, 2019), 1668-1669.

37. David S. Williams, "1 Maccabees," in *The New Interpreter's Study Bible, New Revised Standard Version with Apocrypha* (Nashville, TN: Abingdon Press, 2003), 1551.

38. André LaCocque, "Daniel," in *Global Bible Commentary*, ed. Daniel Patte (Nashville, TN: Abingdon Press, 2004), 253.

39. André LaCocque, "Daniel," in *Global Bible Commentary*, ed. Daniel Patte (Nashville, TN: Abingdon Press, 2004), 253.

40. André LaCocque, "Daniel," in *Global Bible Commentary*, ed. Daniel Patte (Nashville, TN: Abingdon Press, 2004), 256.

41. David S. Williams, "1 Maccabees," in *The New Interpreter's Study Bible, New Revised Standard Version with Apocrypha* (Nashville, TN: Abingdon Press, 2003), 1551.

42. André LaCocque, "Daniel," in *Global Bible Commentary*, ed. Daniel Patte (Nashville, TN: Abingdon Press, 2004), 254.

43. Theodoret of Cyr, "Commentary on Daniel." Translated by Robert C. Hill (Boston: Brill, 2006). In *Writings from the Greco-Roman World* (Atlanta: Society of Biblical Literature, 2001-), 7:123.

44. Jerome. *Commentary on Daniel.* Translated by Gleason L. Archer, Jr. (Grand Rapids, MI: Baker, 1958), 77.

45. Hippolytus, "Scholia on Daniel," in *Hippolytus, Cyprian, Caius, Novatian.* Translated by S.D.F. Salmond. Edited by Alexander Roberts and James Donaldson. 10 vols. 1885-1887 (Reprint, Peabody, MA.: Hendrickson, 1994), 185-191. Quoted in A. Roberts and J. Donaldson, eds. *Ante-Nicene Fathers.* 10 vols. (Buffalo, NY: Christian Literature, 1885-86. Reprint, Grand Rapids, MI: Eerdmans, 1951-56. Reprint, Peabody, MA: Hendrickson, 1994), 5:190.

46. Kenneth Stevenson and Michael Glerup, eds., *"Ezekiel, Daniel,"* Ancient Christian Commentary (Downers Grove, IL: InterVarsity Press, 2008), 242.

47. Daniel 7:25 csb.

48. Daniel 7:25 niv.

49. Jerome. *Commentary on Daniel.* Translated by Gleason L. Archer, Jr. (Grand Rapids, MI: Baker, 1958), 81-82.

50. John Chrysostom, "Interpretatio in Danielem prophetam [Sp]."In *Opera omnia.* Edited by J.P. Migne (Paris: Migne, 1859), 56:231-32, cols. 193-246. Quoted in *Thesaurus Linguae Graecae: Canon of Greek Authors and Works.* 2nd ed. Edited by L. Berkowitz and K. Squiter (Oxford: Oxford University Press, 1986), 2062-209.

51. André LaCocque, "Daniel," in *Global Bible Commentary*, ed. Daniel Patte (Nashville, TN: Abingdon Press, 2004), 256.

52. André LaCocque, "Daniel," in *Global Bible Commentary*, ed. Daniel Patte (Nashville, TN: Abingdon Press, 2004), 256.

53. Grant R. Jeffrey, Daniel 7:13-14 footnote, in *NIV Prophecy Marked Reference Study Bible* (Grand Rapids, MI: Zondervan Publishing House, 1998), 976.

54. Grant R. Jeffrey, Daniel 7:13-14 footnote, in *NIV Prophecy Marked Reference Study Bible* (Grand Rapids, MI: Zondervan Publishing House, 1998), 976.

55. niv.

DANIEL 8

1. Frank Charles Thompson, 4434-Shusan or Susa archeological supplement, in *The Thompson Chain-Reference Bible, New King James Version* (Indianapolis, IN: B.B. Kirkbride Bible Co., Inc., 1997), 1245-1246.

2. nkjv.

3. nkjv.

4. hsb.

5. John F. Walvwoord, *The Prophecy Knowledge Handbook* (Colorado Springs, CO: Victor Books, 1990), 238.

6. John H. Walton, ed., Daniel 8:1 footnote, in *Cultural Backgrounds Study Bible* (Grand Rapids, MI: Zondervan Publishing House, 2017), 1490.

7. John H. Walton, ed., Daniel 8:3-4 footnote, in *Cultural Backgrounds Study Bible* (Grand Rapids, MI: Zondervan Publishing House, 2017), 1490.

8. John D. Barry, Daniel 8:3 footnote, in *NKJV Faithlife Illustrated Study Bible* (Grand Rapids, MI: Zondervan, 2018), 1407.

9. John H. Walton, ed., Daniel 8:5 footnote, in *Cultural Backgrounds Study Bible* (Grand Rapids, MI: Zondervan Publishing House, 2017), 1490.

10. John F. Walvoord, *The Prophecy Knowledge Handbook* (Colorado Springs, CO: Victor Books, 1990), 237.

11. John F. Walvoord, *The Prophecy Knowledge Handbook* (Colorado Springs, CO: Victor Books, 1990), 237.

12. "Wikipedia: Stacy Horn," Wikimedia Foundation, accessed November 23, 2011. https://en.wikipedia.org/wiki/Stacy_Horn.

13. "GOAT: Geographic Online Address Translator," GeoSport, New York City Department of Planning, accessed December 14, 2021, copyright 2021. http://a030-goat.nyc.gov/goat/.

14. John H. Walton, ed., Daniel 8:8 footnote, in *Cultural Backgrounds Study Bible* (Grand Rapids, MI: Zondervan Publishing House, 2017), 1490.

15. John H. Walton, ed., "Greek History," in *Cultural Backgrounds Study Bible* (Grand Rapids, MI: Zondervan Publishing House, 2017), 1493.

16. John H. Walton, ed., Daniel 8:22 footnote, in *Cultural Backgrounds Study Bible* (Grand Rapids, MI: Zondervan Publishing House, 2017), 1492.

17. John F. Walvoord, *The Prophecy Knowledge Handbook* (Colorado Springs, CO: Victor Books, 1990), 237.

18. John H. Walton, ed., Daniel 8:9 footnote, in *Cultural Backgrounds Study Bible* (Grand Rapids, MI: Zondervan Publishing House, 2017), 1491.

19. David Jeremiah, *The Handwriting on the Wall* (Dallas: Word Publishing, 1992), 165.

20. John H. Walton, ed., Daniel 8:10 footnote, in *Cultural Backgrounds Study Bible* (Grand Rapids, MI: Zondervan Publishing House, 2017), 1491.

21. NKJV.

22. John H. Walton, ed., Daniel 8:14 footnote, in *Cultural Backgrounds Study Bible* (Grand Rapids, MI: Zondervan Publishing House, 2017), 1491.

23. John F. Walvoord, *The Prophecy Knowledge Handbook* (Colorado Springs, CO: Victor Books, 1990), 239.

24. "The Daniel 9:24-27 Project: The Framework for Messianic Chronology," Associates for Biblical Research, accessed December 7, 2021. https://biblearchaeology.org/research/the-daniel-9-24-27-project/4362-understanding-the-2-300-evenings-and-mornings-of-daniel-8-14.

25. John H. Walton, ed., Daniel 8:14 footnote, in *Cultural Backgrounds Study Bible* (Grand Rapids, MI: Zondervan Publishing House, 2017), 1491.

26. Grant R. Jeffrey, Daniel 8:14 footnote, in *NIV Prophecy Marked Reference Study Bible* (Grand Rapids, MI: Zondervan Publishing House, 1998), 981.

DANIEL 5

1. John H. Walton, ed., Daniel 5:1 footnote, in *Cultural Backgrounds Study Bible* (Grand Rapids, MI: Zondervan Publishing House, 2017), 1480.

2. Daniel 5:23 NKJV.

3. CSB.

4. John H. Walton, ed., Daniel 5:1 footnote, in *Cultural Backgrounds Study Bible* (Grand Rapids, MI: Zondervan Publishing House, 2017), 1480.

5. John H. Walton, ed., Daniel 5:5 footnote, in *Cultural Backgrounds Study Bible* (Grand Rapids, MI: Zondervan Publishing House, 2017), 1480.

6. Kenneth L. Barker, Daniel 1:6 footnote, in *nasb Study Bible* (Grand Rapids, MI: Zondervan, 1999), 1228.

7. Kenneth L. Barker, Daniel 1:7 footnote, in *nasb Study Bible* (Grand Rapids, MI: Zondervan, 1999), 1228.

8. *Online Etymology Dictionary*, s.v. "Belshazzar," accessed January 10, 2022, https://www.etymonline.com/word/Belshazzar.

9. John H. Walton, ed., Daniel 5:8 footnote, in *Cultural Backgrounds Study Bible* (Grand Rapids, MI: Zondervan Publishing House, 2017), 1481.

10. Lawrence M. Wilis, Daniel 5:25-28 footnote, in *Tanakh Translation, The Jewish Study Bible* (New York, NY: Oxford University Press, 2004), 1652.

11. CSB.

DANIEL 9

1. John H. Walton, ed., Daniel 5:31, 6:28 footnote, in *Cultural Backgrounds Study Bible* (Grand Rapids, MI: Zondervan Publishing House, 2017), 1482, 1485.

2. Jerome, *Commentary on Daniel*. Translated by Gleason L. Archer, Jr. (Grand Rapids, MI: Baker, 1958), 61,63, 69-70, 90.

3. Theodoret of Cyr, "Commentary on Daniel." Translated by Robert C. Hill (Boston: Brill, 2006). In *Writings from the Greco-Roman World* (Atlanta: Society of Biblical Literature, 2001-), 81:1456.

4. Theodoret of Cyr, "Commentary on Daniel." Translated by Robert C. Hill (Boston: Brill, 2006). In *Writings from the Greco-Roman World* (Atlanta: Society of Biblical Literature, 2001-), 81:1456.

5. J.I. Packer, Wayne Grudem, and Ajith Fernando, Introduction to Daniel Commentary, in *Global Study Bible* (Wheaton, IL: Crossway, 2012), 1145-1146.

6. J.I. Packer, Wayne Grudem, and Ajith Fernando, Daniel 9:1-27, in *Global Study Bible* (Wheaton, IL: Crossway, 2012), 1164.

7. "H2532 – Ḥemdâ – Strong's Hebrew Lexicon (KJV)." *Blue Letter Bible*, https://www.blueletterbible.org/lexicon/h2532/kjv/wlc/0-1/.

8. John D. Barry, Daniel 9:25 footnote, in *NKJV Faithlife Illustrated Study Bible* (Grand Rapids, MI: Zondervan, 2018), 141.

9. André LaCocque, "Daniel," in *Global Bible Commentary*, ed. Daniel Patte (Nashville, TN: Abingdon Press, 2004), 256.

10. André LaCocque, "Daniel," in *Global Bible Commentary*, ed. Daniel Patte (Nashville, TN: Abingdon Press, 2004), 256.

11. Global Bible Commentary, chart on page 1167 of Daniel.

12. Kenneth Stevenson and Michael Glerup, eds. *Ancient Christian Commentary; Ezekiel, Daniel* (Downers Grove, IL: InterVarsity Press, 2008), 267.

13. John D. Barry, Daniel 9:24 footnote, in *NKJV Faithlife Illustrated Study Bible* (Grand Rapids, MI: Zondervan, 2018), 1410.

14. Grant R. Jeffrey, "The Vision of the Seventy Weeks," in *NIV Prophecy Marked Reference Study Bible* (Grand Rapids, MI: Zondervan Publishing House, 1998), 986-987.

15. Kenneth Stevenson and Michael Glerup, eds. *Ancient Christian Commentary; Ezekiel, Daniel* (Downers Grove, IL: InterVarsity Press, 2008), 267.

16. Raechel Myers and Amanda Bible Williams, eds. "Timeline: Nehemiah and the Babylonian Captivity," In *He Reads Truth Bible*, (Nashville, TN: Holman Bible Publishers, 2019), 765.

17. Raechel Myers and Amanda Bible Williams, eds. "Timeline: Nehemiah and the Babylonian Captivity," In *He Reads Truth Bible*, (Nashville, TN: Holman Bible Publishers, 2019), 765.

18. Raechel Myers and Amanda Bible Williams, eds. "Timeline: Nehemiah and the Babylonian Captivity," In *He Reads Truth Bible*, (Nashville, TN: Holman Bible Publishers, 2019), 765.

19. J.I. Packer, Wayne Grudem, and Ajith Fernando, Daniel 9:25-26, in *Global Study Bible* (Wheaton, IL: Crossway, 2012), 1166.

20. John H. Walton, ed., Daniel 9:26 footnote, in *NKJV Cultural Backgrounds Study Bible* (Grand Rapids, MI: Zondervan Publishing House, 2017), 1495.

21. J.I. Packer, Wayne Grudem, and Ajith Fernando, "The 70 Weeks of Daniel 9," in *Global Study Bible* (Wheaton, IL: Crossway, 2012), 1167.

DANIEL 6

1. Joshua 1:6-9.
2. Daniel 6:15 NKJV.
3. Daniel 6:16 NKJV.
4. David Loades, "The Early Reception," *The Acts and Monuments Online* (essay), 2011. https://www.john-foxe.org/index_realm_more_gototype_modern_type_essay_book_essay7.html.
5. Daniel 6:23 NKJV.

DANIEL 10

1. Daniel 10:19 nasb.
2. Daniel 10:18 CSB.
3. Didache VII:4.
4. Lawrence M. Wills, Annotations on Daniel 10:13, 20, in *The Jewish Study Bible, Jewish Publication Society Tanakh Translation* (New York, NY: Oxford University Press, 2004), 1662.
5. Matthias Henze, Study notes on Daniel 11:2-45, in *The New Interpreter's Study Bible, New Revised Standard Version with Apocrypha* (Nashville, TN: Abingdon Press, 2003), 1249.
6. Kenneth Stevenson and Michael Glerup, eds., *Ancient Christian Commentary; Ezekiel, Daniel* (Downers Grove, IL: InterVarsity Press, 2008), 276-278, 280.

DANIEL 11

1. Kenneth L. Barker, Daniel 11:2-35 footnote, in *nasb Study Bible* (Grand Rapids, MI: Zondervan, 1999), 1244-1247.
2. Kenneth L. Barker, Daniel 11:1-3 footnote, in *nasb Study Bible* (Grand Rapids, MI: Zondervan, 1999), 1244.
3. Matthias Henze, Study notes on Daniel 11:2-45, in *The New Interpreter's Study Bible, New Revised Standard Version with Apocrypha* (Nashville, TN: Abingdon Press, 2003), 1249.
4. "Ptolemies and Seleucids," chart, *nasb Study Bible* (Grand Rapids, MI: Zondervan, 1999), 1246-1247.
5. *Encyclopaedia Britannica Online*, Britannica, T. ed. "Berenice," accessed on March 19, 2022, https://www.britannica.com/biography/Berenice-daughter-of-Ptolemy-II.
6. Jerome, *Commentary on Daniel*. Translated by Gleason L. Archer, Jr. (Grand Rapids, MI: Baker, 1958), 121-22.
7. Carol A. Newsom, "Daniel," in *Women's Bible Commentary Expanded Edition*, eds. Carol A. Newsom and Sharon H. Ringe (Louisville, Kentucky: Westminster John Knox Press, 1998), 202.
8. *Encyclopaedia Britannica Online*, R. Werner, ed. "Ptolemy I Soter," accessed on March 19, 2022, https://www.britannica.com/biography/Ptolemy-I-Soter.
9. Adele Berlin and Marc Zvi Brettler, "Historical and Geographical Background to the Bible" in *Tanakh Translation, The Jewish Study Bible* (New York, NY: Oxford University Press, 2004), 2058.
10. Kenneth L. Barker, Daniel 11:6 footnote, in *nasb Study Bible* (Grand Rapids, MI: Zondervan, 1999), 1244.
11. Kenneth L. Barker, Daniel 11:7 footnote, in *nasb Study Bible* (Grand Rapids, MI: Zondervan, 1999), 1244.
12. John F. Walvword, *Major Bible Prophecies* (Grand Rapids, MI: Zondervan Publishing House, 1991), 156.
13. Theodoret of Cyr, "Commentary on Daniel." Translated by Robert C. Hill (Boston: Brill, 2006). In *Writings from the Greco-Roman World* (Atlanta: Society of Biblical Literature, 2001-), 7:123.
14. Jerome, *Commentary on Daniel*. Translated by Gleason L. Archer, Jr. (Grand Rapids, MI: Baker, 1958), 120-121.
15. "Ptolemies and Seleucids," chart, *nasb Study Bible* (Grand Rapids, MI: Zondervan, 1999), 1246-1247.
16. Kenneth Stevenson and Michael Glerup, eds., *Ancient Christian Commentary; Ezekiel, Daniel* (Downers Grove, IL: InterVarsity Press, 2008), 286.

17. Matthias Henze, Study notes on Daniel 11:14, 15-17, in *The New Interpreter's Study Bible, New Revised Standard Version with Apocrypha* (Nashville, TN: Abingdon Press, 2003), 1249.

18. Kenneth Stevenson and Michael Glerup, eds., *Ancient Christian Commentary; Ezekiel, Daniel* (Downers Grove, IL: InterVarsity Press, 2008), 286.

19. *Worldhistory.us*, "Cleopatra I Queen of Egypt," accessed on April 20, 2022, https://worldhistory.us/ancient-history/ancient-egypt/cleopatra-i-queen-of-egypt.php.

20. Matthias Henze, Study notes on Daniel 11:18-19, in *The New Interpreter's Study Bible, New Revised Standard Version with Apocrypha* (Nashville, TN: Abingdon Press, 2003), 1250.

21. Kenneth L. Barker, Daniel 11:36 footnote, in *nasb Study Bible* (Grand Rapids, MI: Zondervan, 1999), 1247.

22. Grant R. Jeffrey, Daniel 11:21, 11:25-28 footnote, in *NIV Prophecy Marked Reference Study Bible* (Grand Rapids, MI: Zondervan Publishing House, 1998), 993-994.

23. Matthias Henze, Study notes on Daniel 11:22-28 & 11:29-31, in *The New Interpreter's Study Bible, New Revised Standard Version with Apocrypha* (Nashville, TN: Abingdon Press, 2003), 1250.

24. Matthias Henze, Study notes on Daniel 11:29-31, in *The New Interpreter's Study Bible, New Revised Standard Version with Apocrypha* (Nashville, TN: Abingdon Press, 2003), 1250.

25. Grant R. Jeffrey, Daniel 11:30 footnote, in *NIV Prophecy Marked Reference Study Bible* (Grand Rapids, MI: Zondervan Publishing House, 1998), 994.

26. Kenneth L. Barker, Daniel 11:25 footnote, in *nasb Study Bible* (Grand Rapids, MI: Zondervan, 1999), 1245.

27. Justo L. Gonzalez, *The Story of Christianity* (San Francisco, CA: HarperSanFrancisco, 1984), 83.)

28. Justo L. Gonzalez, *The Story of Christianity* (San Francisco, CA: HarperSanFrancisco, 1984), 86.

29. Justo L. Gonzalez, *The Story of Christianity* (San Francisco, CA: HarperSanFrancisco, 1984), 88.)

30. CSB

31. Jerome, "Commentary on Matthew 24.15," in *Commentary on Matthew 4.24.15* (Turnhout, Belgium, 1969), 77:225-26.

32. Daniel 11:36 CSB.

33. CSB.

34. Daniel 11:10 CSB.

35. Daniel 11:40 CSB.

36. CSB.

37. Jerome, *Commentary on Daniel*. Translated by Gleason L. Archer, Jr. (Grand Rapids, MI: Baker, 1958), 142.

38. Theodoret of Cyr, "Commentary on Daniel." Translated by Robert C. Hill (Boston: Brill, 2006). In *Writings from the Greco-Roman World* (Atlanta: Society of Biblical Literature, 2001-), 7:309-11.

DANIEL 12

1. Revelation 7:15b NKJV.

2. Daniel 12:4b CSB.

3. John 11:27 CSB.

4. John 11:26b CSB.

5. Kenneth L. Barker, Ezekiel 9:4 footnote, in *nasb Study Bible* (Grand Rapids, MI: Zondervan, 1999), 1168.

SCRIPTURE INDEX

OLD TESTAMENT

NEW TESTAMENT

As a child, I am sure my teachers heard me groan when they announced a group project. At the time, it seemed like the teacher had just given permission to my peers to slack and make me do all the work. As an adult, I have learned to appreciate the greatness of teamwork. When one person entrusts to another pieces of a project that better match the other person's skills, the result is a better outcome. I have now learned that this is true in writing a book as well. I am grateful for the team of people who have come alongside *Resilient Faith* to make it better than what it could have been if written, edited, and published by the author alone. Thank you!

Special thanks is given to my editors, Donna Mazzitelli, Jennifer Jas, Nicole Wall, and Megan Jackson. Donna, thank you for being an editor who appreciates "merry dissonance" and respected my need not to fit perfectly into a publishing "box." You were an encouragement from the very beginning. Thank you for showing me the path to publication and making sure that what was in my head was accessible to the reader.

Jennifer, thank you for offering the final proofreading of this manuscript. It is a gift to have someone come with fresh eyes to this manuscript to make sure that everything is correct and to make the author shine. Thank you for adding your professional expertise to this book.

Megan, thank you for taking on the first review of the citations of ancient texts. I know this was a huge task and likely caused you some headaches along the way. Thank you for your patience and your kindness toward me as I shared my fears about not getting this right. Thank you also to Ian Gerdon, who first introduced me to ancient Christian writers and then introduced me to my editor in Europe, Nicole. Nicole, you were a gift to relieve my anxiety; I appreciate your offering your expertise in reviewing and correcting my citations. You went above and beyond to figure out how to format my endnotes and footnotes so that they worked with the overall formatting of the book. Thank you. When I received the manuscript back from you, I had the peace of knowing this book was really going to happen.

Thank you to Christoph Truemper for designing the book cover and Steve Kuhn for formatting the interior of the book to make it appealing to the eye. I am a visual learner. While other people may be more sensitive to correct spelling and punctuation, I have always been more impacted by a book's texture, formatting, and design. There is something special about holding a paper book in hand and flipping through the pages. Thank you for being a part of this project. I appreciate your giving this devotional "curb-appeal."

Thank you also to Rod Caszatt for the logo design. You helped make this project real.

Also, thank you to Bob Malone, Debby Krivanek, Glenn Healy, Lisa Dursky, and Jay Aisenbrey for giving readers' feedback on the manuscript. Thank you to Kirsten Running-Marquardt for encouraging me to use the pandemic shutdown to disciple others through writing and John Kalb for modeling the devotional study of one book of the Bible throughout a month. Finally, thank you to Michael Christensen, Sonya Brown, Kristin Snodgrass, and the Aykurt family for inspiring me with their writing and publishing books of their own.

More appreciation than can be expressed is offered to Dr. Harvey Martin, who inspired many a student to study the Bible more deeply and methodically and to share what they learned creatively with others.

Oh, and I cannot forget—thank you to all of my family members and friends (especially Scott, Grammi, JSTACK, and the Young Life CR crew) who have believed in me, encouraged me, and set an educated and faith-filled Christian example over the years. You have been "church" to me. You are loved and cherished!

If anything said within these pages sounds insightful or wise, all glory goes to the work of God's good Spirit. If anything appears conspiratorial, misleading, or contrived, please forgive the error of my human ways.

S. K. Fine is an ordained and seminary-trained pastor from the Midwest United States. S. K. has served as pastor for a new church plant born from the merger of two older congregations; a Young Life volunteer and area director, serving in both marginalized and multicultural settings; a retreat and lecture series organizer for national elected leaders and Christian influencers; a church transformation consultant; and most recently, a director of discipleship at a downtown church.

S. K.'s mentors are the writers of ancient and classical Christian texts who have been appreciated for generations. This is S. K.'s first devotional commentary.